WHAT'S THAT ALL ABOUT?

Wm. Di'Mon Brown

NuSeason Editions

Harvest Time: What's That All About?
by Wm. Di'Mon Brown

Unless otherwise noted, all Scripture quotations are taken from The King James Version, *Bible Explorer 3.0*. Copyright © 2003 WORDsearch Deluxe Edition. Epiphany Software. All rights reserved.

Scripture references marked "Ampl." are taken from THE AMPLIFIED BIBLE, Copyright © 1954, 1958, 1962, 1964, 1965, 1987 by The Lockman Foundation. All rights reserved. Used by permission. (www.Lockman.org)

Strong's references are taken from the Strong's Exhaustive Concordance of the Bible, *Bible Explorer 3.0*. Copyright © 2003 WORDsearch Deluxe Edition. Epiphany Software. All rights reserved.

Edited by: ASarah Publications
Cover design: Higher Impact Designs

Copyright © 2004 by Wm. Di'Mon Brown
ISBN 0-9755696-0-0
Library of Congress Control Number: 2004106729

This book or parts thereof may not be reproduced in any form, stored in a retrieval system, or transmitted in any form by any means—electronic, mechanical, photocopy, recording, or otherwise—without prior written permission of the publisher, except as provided by United States of America copyright law.

NuSeason Editions
83 Winona Lakes
East Stroudsberg, PA 18301

Life's lessons in a few chapters! It's necessary for all Christians—young and old.

D. Benson • Dardenville, AR

The author gave me insight on why some of my harvest was tied up, as well as practical and relevant things to do to ensure the release of my harvest...Enjoyable, personal, and relevant...further defines some of the principles taught by great prosperity teachers such as Keith Moore, Creflo Dollar, Kenneth Hagin, and Leroy Thompson.

Rev. V. Hughes • Plano, TX

As you read, you actually feel like you are going through a spiritual process, which has steps along the way to guide you.

L. Martinez • New York, NY

...Several times, I called a couple of people and shared some specific passages! A good challenge at the end!

D. Robinson • Southlake, TX

Leading edge and challenging...A very practical book. It followed a path and gave insight and humor in the same breath. It hits the nail on the head, hands you the hammer and the picture, and then watches you do the work it asks of you.

J. Vivenzio • Setauket, NY

In loving memory of our son, Di'Mon Terrell Brown.

Thank You Is Not Enough...

To my Lord, Savior and soon coming King, Jesus Christ, I love You will never be enough to express what I feel for You. Truly, Your love and favor have been more than I will ever understand.

To my wife and best friend, Angela (the most virtuous woman I know), for always knowing this would happen. Many will say, "I'll always be there," but you have proven that you really mean it. To my children, Talima, Di'Mon, Marc'el, and Amoi (my daughter from God), for adding a new level of growth, education, and experience to my life. Only God knows how much I love you all.

To Bishop T.W. Weeks III, for staying on my case to "get this book done!" I love you and thank God for your influence.

To Kenneth Copeland, your series, "Honor from God," amongst others has been a cornerstone in my walk with Christ. For fifteen years, I have been blessed, touched, and bettered by the ministry that God has given you.

To Reverend Jerome Greene, for the foundations in Christ, I kept a lot more than you think.

To Paula and Kim Bryant. Paula, thanks for the time and patience with my first book venture. Kim, thanks for the grace and understanding during this time...God's blessings to your family.

To the whole Joshua and Caleb Ministries/Promise Land Church Outreach FAMILY. Thank you for being an example of what agape (the God kind of love) really is. Fellowship with you is what I live for.

To Pastor Fontaine Richardson, my first born in the faith. You have not only been a son, but a true friend.

Thank you, JCMI department leaders, for taking care of things with such an excellent spirit: Amoi Bray, Stephanie Carpenter, Barbara Carter, Phillip Cooke, Malik and Joy Corbett, Hakeem Gaines, Dietra Harvey, Giselle James, Thomas Moreira, Durron Newman, Andrea Richardson, Lewis Roberts, and Linda Smith.

Many thanks to the men and women who took time to review and provide comments on this book: Debra Benson, Bob Higley, Reverend Vera Hughes, Liz Martinez, Donna Robinson, and John Vivenzio. Your time and thoughts are deeply appreciated.

Contents

Foreword xiii
Introduction xv

Harvest Principle I: Break Ground for the Harvest

  1 What is Prosperity? 22
  2 Name It, Claim It? 24
  3 Noblemen Take Kingdoms......................................26
  4 The Faithful Expand 29
  5 God is Looking for Investors 31
  6 The "IF" Condition 33
  7 According to Your Faith 35

Harvest Principle II: Prepare the Soil

  8 Plowing Comes First 40
  9 What is Plowing?...41
10 The Principles of Plowing 43
11 Start at Ground Zero 45
12 Plow Patiently 46
13 The Three C's 48
14 Put Your Hands to the Plow 51

Harvest Principle III: Set the Right Environment

15 An Open Heaven...58
16 An Open Heart 59
17 A Covenant Relationship 60

Harvest Principle IV: Understand the Sowing Process

18 Sowing is an Investment 66
19 Sowing Yields a Guaranteed Return 67
20 Sowing is Strategic 69
21 Sowing Multiplies and Diversifies 71
22 Sowing…the Measure of the Heart........................73

Harvest Principle V: Understand the Reaping Process

23 Sow…Wait…Reap 80
24 Reap in the Spirit 82
25 Reap in Season 83
26 Refuse to Receive Anything from the Devil 85

Harvest Principle VI: Guard Against Losses

27 No Seed, No Godly Harvest 92
28 Guard Against an Impatient Heart 93
29 Guard Against Laziness 98
30 Small Seed, Small Harvest 99
31 Guard Against Selfishness 101
32 Guard Against Carelessness 104
33 Guard Against Fear 107
34 Guard Against Sowing in Unfertile Ground 109
35 Guard Against Sowing in Unfavorable Conditions 111

Harvest Principle VII: Discern Your Harvest

36 Why One Hundredfold? 116
37 How Big is the Harvest? 118
38 Is it Time to Reap? 121
39 Where is the Harvest? 123
40 How Much Can You Reap? 127
41 Don't Sleep through Your Harvest 129
42 Go In and Possess 133

Harvest Principle VIII: Take Your Full Harvest

43 Declare Victory in the Spirit 140
44 Put Your Feet Down 141
45 Don't Lose Heart 142
46 Be Willing to Share 144
47 Help Someone Else to Reap 145
48 Know It's Never Too Late 147
49 Step Out and Find Out 148
50 Never Compromise with the Enemy 149
51 Rise to Greatness in God 151

52	Distribute the Surplus 153
53	It's Yours for the Taking 154
54	Walk in Your God-given Authority 156

Harvest Principle IX: Sustain Your Land

55	How Much Ground Are You Going to Keep? 162
56	Let the Soil Rest 163
57	Lift Up Your Eyes 164
58	Keep Your Head Covered 166
59	Be Instant…in Every Season 168
60	Keep Reaching Out 169
61	Let Your Roots Go Deep 171
62	Fight the "Good Fight" 173

Recommended Resources

Foreword

When my husband first started ministering to me about the *Harvest Time* message, it was hard for me to accept. We had been coming through very difficult times, and frankly, I didn't want to hear it. I had known my husband for a long time...even before he was saved, so whenever he'd try to talk to me I'd be thinking, *I'm saved just like you are. The fact that you hear from God doesn't mean that He has to tell me things through you!* Whenever he would try to share what God was teaching him, I'd listen with a polite detachment hoping that he wouldn't say any more than was absolutely necessary. I also wasn't putting any of these truths into practice. In short, I was working hard at being an unsubmissive wife.

During this time in our lives my husband was beginning to be richly blessed. God was doing powerful things in his ministry. Whenever I watched Di'Mon minister, I would see people's reactions when he'd pray for them and give them a prophetic word. Many of these people came to me later saying that my husband had been "right on point" when delivering the word and that the things God had spoken through him had come to pass. Yet in all of this, nothing was happening to me! I told the Lord, "Something is definitely wrong; why am I not getting blessed?"

I went to my husband and asked, "Why is God prospering you? You talk to people and prophesy to them, and I keep seeing things happen for them, but it's not happening for me." Then one morning during my prayer time the Lord spoke the word, "Rebellious." I said, "Lord, I'm not rebellious." He said, "Yes, you are...you are not committed to your husband." Defensively, I said, "But, Lord, I cook, clean, and do everything that a submitted wife should do." He said..."You still aren't submissive, and you are hindering the blessings in your household."

Those words brought an awakening in my life—because I thought I had been doing all of the right things! Something in me had to change. I repented to the Lord and asked what I needed to do differently; I prayed, quoted scriptures, confessed the Word, and did all of the things that I knew to do. Still, nothing happened.

Not long after that, the Lord reminded me that I was still not operating in true submission. This time, I searched the Bible for answers until I finally could identify what was lacking. Turning to my best friend, my husband, I received the counsel that I needed.

Harvest Time: What's That All About?

At that time, Di'Mon wasn't a pastor, yet he was very knowledgeable about the Bible. As he taught me, I could feel changes taking place in my heart. I was amazed. Through my husband, God was literally washing me with the water of His Word!

The Lord often has to take us through "cleansing processes" that may require drastic changes in our thinking. But if we repent when He deals with us and then obey what He tells us to do, in return, He will give us "hearing ears." That's what happened to me. As this washing process continued, I recognized and acknowledged the deep things within me that had been blocking God's blessings in my life. That's when God began imparting the life-transforming message of *Harvest Time* into my heart.

Eventually, both my husband and I sensed deep changes in our attitudes and perceptions about our life. We made the decision that, together, we would apply these harvesting principles and "do things right" in the eyes of the Lord. I am so happy to say that everything changed with that decision.

When my husband began teaching *Harvest Time* to our members, I discovered how easy it seemed to be for people to relate it to their day-to-day lives. Even now, I often hear that because he puts each principle into such simple terms anyone can understand it—and I believe you will have the same experience. Now, I teach a class for our members to explain how these harvesting principles can apply while working through one's everyday budget. I have found that most of the students, much like Di'Mon and me, had been praying and confessing the Word, but they hadn't gone before God in repentance or changed their financial patterns. It's exciting to see many of these believers getting the same results that Di'Mon and I saw manifest in our lives.

I firmly believe that you will be richly blessed through reading and applying the principles of *Harvest Time*. As you read, I encourage you to let go, listen to the Lord, and follow His instructions. So many people have heard this message and shared how their lives have been blessed. Now, it's your turn. As you walk through each step of the harvesting process, I know that your life will never be the same.

Harvest Time: What's That All About?

Introduction

When God birthed this harvesting message in me, I was younger in the Lord and loving Him to the best of my ability. I was tithing, going to church three days a week, and doing all of the things that I thought were supposed to bring biblical prosperity; yet at best, I was reaping little to nothing according to biblical principles. In fact, I was reaping terrible circumstances. My family was homeless. In desperation I cried out, "What's wrong, Lord?" He spoke to my heart that He would bring me to an understanding of true prosperity.

As I continued seeking the Lord, I discovered that the first and most prosperous thing any person could ever do in this life is to receive Jesus Christ as Lord and Savior. True prosperity is not found in the pocket or purse...it is found in the spirit. It is found in knowing that Jesus died and was resurrected on your behalf.

Another truth about prosperity became clear to me when I realized the true value of being filled with the Holy Ghost. I came to understand that it hadn't been given for me to simply speak in tongues, but to endue me with supernatural power to be the Lord's witness. Slowly but surely, that understanding became a reality in my life.

During this process, I began to search for teachings on how to be blessed and to prosper. The first tape series I came across was called, "The Laws of Prosperity," by Kenneth Copeland. That title struck me because I didn't think prosperity operated according to spiritual laws. I had been operating in the understanding that prosperity hinged on the fact that God, deciding He liked me and that I had suffered long enough, would throw me a dollar.

About that same time someone gave me a tape series by Keith Moore called, "Rules of Reaping." This contained even more laws and principles of prosperity. I rounded it up by listening to another series by Kenneth Copeland called, "Honor from God"—not the honor that comes from man, but that which comes from God alone. Over the next year and a half, I wouldn't listen to anything other than those tape series. I would finish one series and then go on to the next, sometimes listening to each tape three or four times. I wanted to be certain these truths were engrained in my spirit.

As I studied and brought what I was learning before the Lord in prayer, He began to reveal a law to me that I had never heard anyone teach, and it's critical to the harvesting process (this is covered in Harvest Principle II). Prior to receiving this revelation, I had been giving without acknowledging this law and that's why my harvest had been unfruitful. As I worked through this principle and was able to distinguish the various stages involved in harvesting, God birthed the message of *Harvest Time* within me.

It didn't take long for me to start relating the laws to my financial situation and the fact that I was still homeless. This is why one of the first things that I counsel people to do when they receive a revelation from God is to not relate it to where they are, but instead, to where God is taking them. His thoughts and ways are higher than ours, so it can be somewhat frightening and overwhelming to receive a word from God if you try to understand it according to what you currently know instead of believing by faith what God is revealing.

Again, at the time I was receiving this revelation I was doing everything that the faith and prosperity preachers were teaching: I was giving, confessing, claiming, binding, and loosing. To be honest, I can't say that these methods weren't effective, because I did see some small results—but at best they were proving to be only temporary fixes. Each breakthrough lasted long enough to get me by until the next time I got into financial trouble and needed another fix.

My experience was similar to stories I've heard about people who are overweight that have tried a popular diet hoping to reach a certain goal. Then when they didn't maintain the same eating habits after they had lost the unwanted pounds, they found themselves squeezing back into the same clothes they had worn before the diet. In the end result, learning to eat the right foods can take off unwanted pounds, but to keep those pounds off, there must be a total change of diet and lifestyle.

It is a well-known saying that insanity can be defined as doing the same thing the same way you've always done it, yet expecting a different result.

Spiritually speaking, I had learned what to do and confess in order to get what turned out to be an occasional financial breakthrough. Then afterwards, I would sink right back to the mindset that had gotten me in debt. As a result, we were doing all that we knew to do in our giving and were still living in poverty. Every time God gave us a breakthrough, we'd waste the money and find ourselves broke again.

On two different occasions, we experienced the humiliation of being evicted. The first time it happened was in 1994…and it was a terrible experience. My family was thrown out of our apartment into the streets in the midst of the biggest snowstorm that New York City had ever had. The day that snowstorm began, the Marshall was tossing us out and taking our belongings. Even worse than that, we were only at the beginning of our deepest times of trouble.

Harvest Time: What's That All About?

For a while, we stayed with my sister but having five additional people in her home proved to be too much. So without a home of our own, we were forced to separate our family. No one had enough space for all of us to stay together. From that point on, I stayed with my mother while my wife and kids lived elsewhere. My wife's family and many others were calling me a bum, saying that I didn't want to support my family. I went through a great deal of emotional pain, because I knew what a Christian husband should do; yet my family was in this terrible situation. This weighed heavily on my heart.

As strange as it may sound, I continued to tithe during our homeless period. When we received welfare checks I would literally pay a tithe from our food stamps. While I was doing this, people all around me were saying, "You need to feed your family and stop this religious stupidity." No one seemed to understand what I was learning and starting to believe in my spirit from embracing the harvesting message.

Still, in trying to digest these truths about prosperity I hadn't yet grasped the principle (mentioned earlier) that changed my life. I was receiving new revelations from the tapes, but I still had not received my own Rhema word from the Lord. Then it came. As I developed an understanding in this vital area, I realized it had to be done at the beginning of the process—and that's why the other principles hadn't been working in my life.

As my understanding deepened, my first step was to admit that I had been putting my dreams and ambitions ahead of taking care of my wife and family. The Lord really had to deal with me about that issue. I had perceived in error that because I was doing everything *for* them, it didn't matter what the decisions I made were doing *to* them. I tried to defend myself by saying, "Lord, I mean well," but God started revealing to me that "meaning well" and "doing well" are two different things.

I had to stop "meaning well" and start "doing well." This meant that I had to make the decision to let go of my business, or I'd lose everything else. I had to determine, first and foremost, that I wanted to feed and take care of my family—even if it meant leaving behind every dream I had ever received from God. Now, I don't have that problem. My family comes first.

The second time we were homeless, I went to my wife and told her, "This will never happen again! You have my word that I will take care of you." From that moment, we came into divine agreement and everything started turning around for us. We've been in forward motion ever since. We haven't had a single "down" moment financially since 1997—not one!

Harvest Time: What's That All About?

That same year, we established the church and held our first service in our living room. It was definitely a process. I had worked for the same company for eight months, so when God told me to start the church, I tried to reason with Him: we had a good car, and for the first time were paying our bills on time. It only made sense that I should stay on that job. I even reminded God that according to the scriptures, a man who doesn't take care of his family is "…worse than an infidel" (see 1 Timothy 5:8). The Lord replied, "Okay, go ahead, but I told you to quit your job and start the church." So that's what I did.

For several months after leaving my job it looked like God was sending me straight back to the poverty level that I had come from…but it wasn't long before I realized that He was just "setting me up" for my next assignment, a position in computer technology. God used that job to continue establishing my family as we continued following Him in ministry. Two years later, we started a Bible study at St. John's University. Now, Joshua and Caleb Ministries, Inc./Promise Land Church Outreach is a young, vibrant congregation in the Bronx, New York. God has continued to bless and multiply the ministry, and I am eternally grateful.

Remember that as you learn the principles of harvesting, you must keep first things first. God's first priority is to prosper your spirit and soul, because you will get a harvest from whatever you've planted…financially or otherwise. A "harvest" is based on what you sow with or without the intention of reaping—that means you can reap good, bad, and unintentional harvests.

By unintentional I mean those ungodly seeds that you sow without thinking about the results you're going to reap. If I were to make up another term for this type of harvest, I'd call it a "poverty harvest"— because as a result of your unbelief (that causes you to either be in error, inactive, or delayed in any area of giving), the negative results will come whether you're trying to make them happen or not.

Here's the good news. God is not a respecter of persons. In other words, if He'll help me to overcome my lack of understanding and deliver my family from bondage, He'll gladly do the same for you. You simply need to learn how to identify and activate the biblical principles of sowing and reaping. I believe the *Harvest Time* message will help you in this process. If you let God lead you through the harvesting principles as you read this book, I believe that you will soon be able to pray and declare a mighty harvest in your life that will extend far beyond the financial realm.

Take a moment now and pray with me…

"It is my prayer, Lord, that this book will not only become a source of good reading, but also of encouragement, instruction, and direction for those who may be in the same place that I was in; doing all that they know to do and continuing to stand, yet not receiving the manifestation of what they've been believing for in Christ. It is my prayer that not another soul will die and leave this planet with unfulfilled dreams and unrealized visions.

"Lord, I pray that my brother or sister who is reading this book will not live with a sense of discouragement or lack that comes from misunderstanding the promises You have sovereignly placed in Your Word. Hosea 4:6 tells us that we, Your people, are destroyed for lack of knowledge. So, Lord, I pray that the knowledge contained in this book will work together with any insights that my brother or sister has already gleaned from Your Word and Spirit, and that it will transform every area of his or her life.

"Father God, I pray that You would allow a deep spiritual development to take place through this teaching regarding the entire harvesting process, and that the rest of my brother or sister's days will be marked by unbridled fulfillment in the things of God…in Jesus' name. Amen."

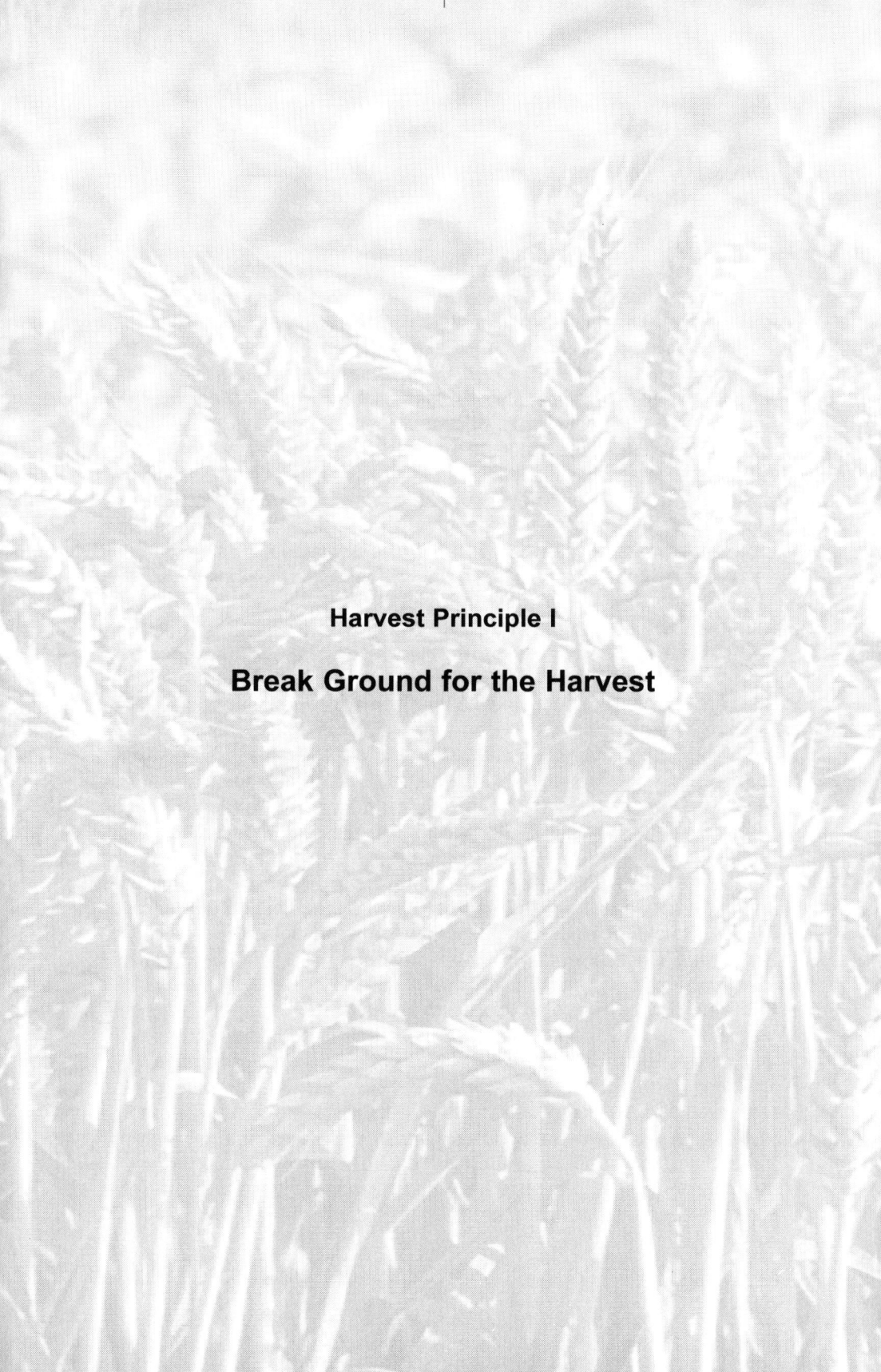

Harvest Principle I

Break Ground for the Harvest

- 1 -
What is Prosperity?

People usually equate the blessings of God with "stuff," so when they think about receiving from the Lord, they naturally assume that He's going to give them some "material" thing. This mindset can be expressed by an old saying, "Give a man a fish and you'll feed him for a day. Teach a man to fish and you'll feed him for a lifetime." The problem with seeking God just to get a "thing" is that it puts you in the position to have a fish, but not to become a fisherman.

Genesis 1:26 says that God made us in His image and in His likeness. God is a spirit. While we know it's not possible to "look like" a spiritual image, we are all spiritual beings that are clothed in a physical "house." In our spirit man, every believer looks like God. In the natural sense, this means we have attributes or ways that cause people to recognize that God is in us. Being made in His likeness means to "be like" the Lord—so we're supposed to "look like" and "be like" our Father in heaven.

In other words, you should be the best interpretation or impression of what God would look like to somebody who doesn't know Him. My son, Marc'el, doesn't look exactly like me, but he looks enough like me that you'd know he's my son.

When Jesus said in John 14:12, "And the works that I do you shall do also, and greater works…" He was saying, "Anything I do and have done you can do." He went on to say, "…and greater works than these shall you do." Some think that when Jesus said we'd do "greater works," He meant there would be more people on the earth, so as a result, we could do more things in more places. I don't totally subscribe to this, because God has never been stuck in one geographic region. He can be anywhere He wants to be, anytime He wants to be there. I believe that when Jesus talked about "greater works," He was talking about the magnitude of what He did.

First of all, Jesus didn't do anything until after John baptized Him in the Jordan River and the Holy Spirit came upon Him. (I have seen television programs where Jesus was walking around as a little boy healing people. That's not scripturally accurate; that's somebody's creative license.) The Bible does say that Jesus had great wisdom as a child, as was evidenced in the story where his parents found Him reasoning among adults in the temple—but there's no record of Him actually performing a miracle until after He was baptized and the Holy Spirit descended upon Him like a dove (see Matthew 3:16).

That's when the miracles began. His first miracle took place at a party. You probably know the story. Things were dying down a bit and when they ran out of wine, they went to Jesus' mother. She said, "Go, do what He says…" Jesus turned the water into wine and said, "Let's keep the party going." Now, think about it. Jesus wasn't stumbling around (like they often portray Him on television programs) looking depressed, rag-tag, and broke. If He had, who would have wanted to follow Him? If Jesus could make wine from water, He definitely wasn't walking around in ripped up clothes saying, "Follow Me, I am the way."

People are the same today as they've always been. Even in the Bible, the Israelites wouldn't line up to follow a depressed, busted-up-looking loser. People want to follow someone like Michael Jordan, or whoever else seems to be "large" in society. They want to follow a person that they perceive to be where they want to be, or to have what they want to have.

Peter and the other disciples were fishermen, the equivalent of modern day truck drivers. Do you think it was a light thing for these men to drop their businesses and follow Jesus? I don't. Jesus had to represent something "large" enough to them that they said, "I'm willing to leave my means of support behind." There was something charismatic about Him that made them say, "I'll leave everything and follow You."

Looking for blessings with a focus on "things" isn't what God intended. He wants to reveal His blessings through us…which ties in to Matthew 6:33, "But seek ye first the kingdom of God, and his righteousness; and all these things shall be added…" Let's consider this. If something is to be "added," then it's not primary. And that's what we've made it. We've made financial prosperity the "thing." Jesus put prosperity in the right perspective. He said it would be "added" if the primary substance was there.

A building is only as good as its foundation. So if the foundation is material blessing, then when you try to build on it, it's going to crumble. Nobody ever brings you into their house and says, "Check out my foundation…don't you like that concrete? It's cracking, but it's a good foundation."

Not me. I don't want to show you the foundation; I want to show you my house. I want to show you the stuff in my house. I want to rush you through the garage…because I want you to see the "things" that are on top of the foundation—even though the foundation is primary for everything else to exist. Matthew 6:33 clearly says, "Seek ye first the kingdom and His righteousness…" meaning that a right standing relationship with God is our foundation. Now, you could take that to mean, "You've got to live right and be right." This is true; but it's still secondary.

You can't *live right* and *be right* if you don't have a sound foundation. That's why some people keep falling, stumbling, and crumbling—because their foundation is faulty. They're trying to "build up" on something that they haven't "built down" first. A foundation determines how high a building can be built. The higher the building, the deeper and wider the foundation has to be. You can't take a building and make it one hundred and fifty feet high and only eight feet square. The foundation must be broadened to deal with the height. Spiritually speaking, this is what happens when believers simply pop off a few "bless me" scriptures thinking that's a foundation. What happens when they want to build mansions on top of it?

- 2 -

Name It, Claim It?

Sometimes you can bump your head enough times and get a clue. Believers don't usually go to their deathbed nasty, bitter, and cantankerous. I don't understand how a Christian could be bitter. That's an oxymoron! How could you be an unforgiving/forgiven person? The problem with unforgiving believers is they have an unstable foundation. They haven't truly accepted forgiveness; therefore, they can't forgive. If you really know you've been forgiven, then it's easy for you to forgive others. To me, this is a primary reason why there are so many issues in the body of Christ…and also why many believers aren't operating in the principles of blessing regarding sowing and reaping.

What usually happens is that people with either no foundation or a faulty foundation will go out and start trying to claim "things." They hear the latest sayings like, "I'll never be broke another day in my life…" and then start trying to build on them. If there's no foundation, there can be no building. Don't get me wrong. I'm not against these teachings; but when you try to operate in them with no spiritual foundation, you'll end up just claiming stuff…and you won't get a harvest.

Let me say something for the record. If you don't have a foundation, don't start binding and rebuking the devil—because he won't just get up and leave. If you start a fight, he'll meet you in the ring to see if you really mean what you say. For example, you'll walk up to the

Harvest Principle I: Break Ground for the Harvest

devil and say, "The wealth of the sinner is laid up for the just...I rebuke you. Release that money to me now." He won't say, "Okay, here..." and hand over the money. He'll say, "Let's see if you really believe what you said," because the enemy knows when you don't. Then if he cracks you over the head one time, you'll go running to your pastor saying, "Oh, Pastor, pray for me. I don't know if I've heard the Lord or not."

Roy Jones, Jr. is one of the best boxers that I've ever seen, but he took a couple of good blows in the face before he won. Just because you lost a round doesn't mean you'll lose the fight! But this is the reality of a "foundation-less" person...he or she is always fighting against the devil. The question is: *How did he get possession of your things anyway?* Most Christians have to fight because he knows they don't believe, and that opens the door to his influence. When you know your authority in Christ, you don't have to fight the devil.

When people have a light understanding of foundation, they start claiming stuff and it usually doesn't come to pass. It can also end up bringing more problems than they had before they started claiming. Has this ever happened to you? Have you found yourself on your knees before God saying, "God, where are my blessings? I pay my tithes. I give. I attend church...I'm doing the right things." Let me tell you: If you were doing the right thing, it would be working! God is not a man that He should lie; His Word works all the time (see Numbers 23:19). God doesn't take vacations; He constantly watches over His Word to perform it.

Christians also tend to make up excuses when we step out to do something and it doesn't go the way we think it should. We say, "Well, maybe God didn't want me to do that." Don't you think God had sense enough to tell you that before you started messing with it? Yes! But that's your excuse to quit, that's your reason to give up. You should have gone to God for direction before you stepped out. Luke 14:28–30 says, "For which of you, intending to build a tower, sitteth not down first, and counteth the cost, whether he have *sufficient* to finish *it*? Lest haply, after he hath laid the foundation, and is not able to finish *it*, all that behold *it* begin to mock him, Saying, This man began to build, and was not able to finish."

This is why you could be in trouble with "things" you already have, especially if you got them without counting the cost. You can't buy a car only considering the monthly payment. You have to look at the cost of insurance, as well as other related costs. Maybe you applied for a credit card because the company said you could have it and then charged it up thinking, *I can make the minimum monthly payments*—not realizing that minimum monthly payment doesn't touch what you've really spent; you're just paying interest. So you end up paying ten thousand dollars for something that actually cost twenty-five hundred. That's an example of building on no foundation.

If you're in this debt cycle, you're borrowing somebody else's money at a very high price. And some of these credit card companies have interest rates hiked up to twenty-four or twenty-eight percent. Twenty-eight percent is usury—that's like being a legal loan shark! These companies have found a way to make something legal that's definitely illegal from a biblical perspective. Why do you think this nation is in the trouble it's in? The Bible makes it crystal clear that God despises usury.

The bottom line is, you can't just name it and claim it. You need to build on a solid foundation. And that foundation is *in you*.

- 3 -

Noblemen Take Kingdoms

Let's look at the nineteenth chapter of Luke. Jesus said, "Therefore, a certain nobleman went into a far country to receive for himself a kingdom, and to return. And he called his ten servants, and delivered them ten pounds, and said unto them, Occupy till I come" (vv. 12–13). I want you to notice something, because we usually skip over "little details" to get to the story. *Noblemen* go forward to take kingdoms. Noblemen seek kingdoms and have servants.

Many of God's people are claiming blessings, but noblemen seek kingdoms. Noblemen are in the place to employ. If you're *the head and not the tail, above and not beneath*, according to Deuteronomy 28:13, then you should have the mentality of an owner.

Now, watch what happened in this story. Luke 19:14 says, "But his citizens hated him, and sent a message after him, saying, We will not have this *man* to reign over us." He had employees, but when he went to get another kingdom they said, "We don't want him; we want him out." Let's keep reading, "And it came to pass, that when he was returned, having received the kingdom, then he commanded these servants to be called unto him, to whom he had given the money, that he might know how much every man had gained by trading" (v. 15).

Harvest Principle I: Break Ground for the Harvest

When God positions you and gives you something, He does it so that you might take that something and make something more with it. Many of us have been trained to merely survive…to get a paycheck, pay our bills, and be satisfied until the next paycheck comes. But Jesus was talking about a "nobleman." If somebody comes to me and says, "Pastor, I can't pay my bills. Could you loan me some money?" I usually say, "You're asking me to put you in debt and I'm not going to do that." Either I'm going to give it to you or you're not getting it.

Too often, people ask for money to pay off a debt, not to invest in something that will better their condition—because that's how we've been trained to live. The church has to get out of this, "Give me a blessing" mode. "Give me a car that makes me happy for a while until it starts rusting." Where are we, as kingdom people, when we're not becoming noblemen who are seeking to purchase or to build a kingdom? We have an employee's mentality, yet we want to claim things so that someone wealthy might look at us and think that we're prosperous. I've got news for you. The average rich man isn't going to be impressed with your gospel, especially if you're trying to present it from an "I am blessed" perspective.

We need to change our foundation. We need to rip up the foundation we've grown accustomed to that says, "Let's find a decent job and pay some bills." The reason God hasn't moved many believers into greatness is that they are still not seeking greatness. They are *confessing* greatness, but not seeking it—because when they pray God knows that what they're praying for isn't a means to improve. It's merely a means to sustain.

God will make new levels of the anointing available to you as you seek to use them. He doesn't push things on you for which you haven't prayed. So if you're praying for an upkeep, but confessing wealth and prosperity, my question to you is, "What are you doing to continue to manifest wealth and prosperity; not only in your life, but also in the lives of those around you?"

I've heard that one of the richest men in the world once said, "I'd rather have one percent of a hundred people's efforts than a hundred percent of my own." That's a noble mentality. The problem for many is that we don't like sharing. We don't want anybody to become prosperous before we do, because we want to be the ones that give somebody else a dollar. While we're confessing greatness, and at the same time not seeking nobility, we're withholding blessings from others because we're thinking if prosperity ever comes…we want it first.

Remember this: Nothing of any real substance in the kingdom has been built without a unified effort.

When people come to me saying, "I have a business idea…" and I start talking to them about business; if I mention partnership they freak out. "Oh, you want to be a partner? I just thought you were going to loan me the money." They'd rather for me to loan them the money to get started, and then struggle being in debt to me than to offer me partnership with a small percentage. They'd rather be in debt than to gain a partner that might add an element of victory to what they're doing. I've asked people, "Which is better? Fifty percent of one million dollars or one hundred percent of a hundred dollars?"

Many Christians don't think that way. We want to say, "It's mine. I'll let you work for me, but it's mine." This takes me back to the nobleman in Luke nineteen. His people didn't like him because they didn't want to work for him. They didn't want to merely manage his money; they wanted to partner in the kingdom. This is what happens when you don't make people part of the process. When you don't offer them ownership, they'll work to get your money—not to build your business.

This isn't normal pulpit material, but I believe the Bible is revealing what we've missed. We've become so accustomed to acquiring things that we don't understand how to build the kingdom. A bunch of stuff is just a bunch of stuff; but when you put yourself in the place where you begin to create opportunities for other people, they'll rally behind what you're doing and build it with you. Give people a job and they'll work for you. Give them a percentage and they'll work for the business. There's a big difference.

If you're building a dream and trying to make it only your thing, the commitment of the people you bring in will be low. Every time somebody comes to our church they say, "Wow, you've got this house organized so well; you really keep it in order." I'm always quick to respond, "No, that isn't me. We have ministers that handle that area. I just make sure to bring a good word." I've made it everybody's ministry, not my ministry that other people attend. So everybody works diligently because they feel that they're an important part of what's happening at the church…and they are.

There are always people who attend church but they don't want to work; they simply want to build their own thing—and that's fine. That doesn't upset me. My point is this: If you have a selfish mentality, it's keeping people out who would otherwise want to sow into what you're doing. When you don't let people have a part in what God has anointed you to build, then you're turning them into slaves. If you're truly seeking a kingdom, then others have to be a part of it.

- 4 -
The Faithful Expand

Let's continue with the story from Luke nineteen, "Then came the first, saying, Lord, thy pound hath gained ten pounds. And he said unto him, Well, thou good servant: because thou hast been faithful in a very little, have thou authority over ten cities" (vv. 16–17). He didn't say because this servant was faithful with little, he'd bless him with a little bit more. He said that he had earned the right to have authority over cities. All God asks for is a little bit of faithfulness and He'll give you a grand promotion. Think about it. If you're getting *small* promotions, it's because you haven't been faithful with *little*.

Let me put it this way. Don't keep asking God to bless you with more money, when you still don't want to tithe with the little bit that you have. God has blessed me because of what I've given in obedience to His Word. Jesus made the statement, "...It is more blessed to give than to receive" (Acts 20:35). It took me a long time to relate to that one. I'd say, "Okay, I understand the giving thing, but Lord, I need *some things*—so I don't see how You're telling me it's better to give than to receive. I just don't see how that makes sense."

Then I started to understand a vital principle: When you become a storehouse, God stocks you. Like the nobleman in Luke 19, He identifies investors and then multiplies resources back to them. I'm the same way. I don't give to squanderers. When I give, "It's for the needy, not the greedy." To me, *needy* doesn't describe somebody that's mismanaged his or her money and is now about to be evicted. You might say, "But Pastor, you have to take care of the poor and the homeless." I agree...but sometimes people are poor and homeless because that's what they desire. No matter what you give them, they'll go through it and be poor again next month.

When you see a homeless person there's a reason he's homeless. He doesn't need money, he needs some instruction and information; because without it, he'll take the "things" you give him and use them in the way to which he's become accustomed. To really help somebody, you shouldn't merely give something to get that individual out of the trouble that he or she has continued to create. Give that person an opportunity to invest—a means to do something greater.

Two ladies at our church came to me one day and said, "We have this dream to open a day care center." It had been prophesied to them years before. They explained, "We want to do this thing. We've been seeking the Lord about it and have been looking for some property." As I was sitting there, the Lord said to me, "Invest in this; put some money into this. Go in with them on the building; do this thing with them." So I said, "That's fine. Instead of just trying to find a place for the day care, let's find a place that we can turn into a church and a day care center." They were so excited. "That's what the Lord showed us!"

Now, that's investing—because it empowered them with an opportunity to bring a vision to pass. Merely helping people to pay rent because they took their rent money and went Christmas shopping is not investing.

Let's go back to Jesus' story in Luke 19, "...Well, thou good servant: because thou hast been faithful in a very little, have thou authority over ten cities. And the second came, saying, Lord, thy pound hath gained five pounds. And he said likewise to him, Be thou also over five cities. And another came, saying, Lord, behold, *here is* thy pound, which I have kept laid up in a napkin" (vv. 17–20). This servant basically said, "I wrapped up what you gave me, put it in the Tupperware bowl...and here it is. I didn't spend it; in fact, I didn't do anything with it." In other words, he didn't invest it. Why?

Verse 21 starts out with three significant words, "For I feared..." Most believers don't ever see a great manifestation of God in their lives because they're afraid of doing something wrong—so as a result, they don't do anything. They get trapped into faulty thinking like, *Maybe God doesn't want me to be blessed because He feels I might be filled with pride and run off chasing women or something. Maybe I'd do the wrong thing and use drugs. Wealth isn't good for people; if you get rich, it can spoil you.*

Proverbs 1:32 clearly says, "...the prosperity of fools shall destroy them." Wealth doesn't corrupt people; wealth gives people license to show who they really are. Let's say a certain man is broke and doesn't have anything going for him. All he does is lust after women and get high. When this man gets a lot of money, he's going to chase a lot of women and stay high all the time—because it will give expression to who he really is. People don't start thinking crazy after they get money; they were crazy already...but they were too poor to act on it. Nobody cared about their crazy thinking when they were broke; but when they got money, it created the opportunity for them to display their true character.

On a positive note, I'm a giver. I love giving. I love blessing people. What happens to me when I get a lot of money? I do a lot more blessing and a lot more giving—because that's who I am. You follow? Money gives license and expression to who you really are. So why are God's people so afraid of money?

This explains what happened with the three servants. When they received their master's money, it gave expression to who they really were. According to what was already in their hearts, each one took what the master had given and did something with it. Then each brought the return from their efforts back to the master.

By now, you must realize that the nobleman represents God. What is God speaking to you from this story? If God sees that you would be faithful to expand (or increase) what He gives you in order to bring Him a return, He'll give you cities.

- 5 -

God is Looking for Investors

Why did the nobleman give them cities? Why didn't he just give them a lot of stuff? A lot of Christians understand this verse to mean: "If you're faithful with little, God's going to give you a Mercedes, houses, and all kinds of stuff for you to enjoy." That's not what the nobleman was seeing. He was identifying investors; motivators who would take things and make things happen. I can just hear what he was thinking, *If I give them cities, they're going to turn them into empires; not throw their feet up in the chair and eat potato chips.*

God is looking for kingdom builders. He's seeking those who will take what He gives them and create opportunities to make life better for somebody else. So if you're going around with this *me, me, me...I claim stuff for me* attitude, that's why you're not getting anything—because you're not a faithful servant. If God were to give you something, you'd either destroy it or hide it in the Tupperware bowl and give it back saying, "See, God, I'm a good Christian. I didn't mess up what You gave me." That might be true...but you didn't do anything with it, either.

As a Pastor, God has given me sons and daughters as part of a covenant family. If I were to start exploiting and taking advantage of them, it wouldn't take long to see the results. Most of them would be up and out of the church as fast as they could go. And I'd be sitting there saying, "Well, they must not have been servants of the Lord. They were never really supposed to be here anyway." On the other hand, God would be telling me, "No, you perverted what I gave you."

When God gives you something, He expects you to steward it. He expects you to keep it before Him in purity according to the Word. Once you break that covenant, God is no longer obligated to let you keep it. He'll take that thing back from you. You can't say, "God, I know what You promised and I'm standing on it," when you took what He gave you and misused it. God won't let you hold Him hostage with a promise that you have broken. You must abide in the Lord and His Word, and repent quickly if you fall into sin.

People don't want to hear this kind of teaching, but it's the truth. If I were to enter a covenant with you and promise that I'd never do a certain thing; then you said to me, "As long as you keep your word to me, whatever I have is yours," that would seal it. If I turned around and did the thing that I promised never to do, would you still be obligated to continue giving me whatever you have? Absolutely not!

Proverbs 19:29 says, "Judgments are prepared for scoffers, and stripes for the backs of [self-confident] fools." On the other hand, 1 Corinthians 2:9 promises—"...What eye has not seen and ear has not heard and has not entered into the heart of man, [all that] God has prepared (made and keeps ready) for those who love Him [who hold Him in affectionate reverence, promptly obeying Him and gratefully recognizing the benefits He has bestowed]" (Ampl.).

Always remember: Whatever God gives you shouldn't stop with you. Multiply the little you have and you'll be given much in return. Proverbs 11:29 promises, "The liberal soul shall be made fat: and he that watereth shall be watered also himself." Do your best to build the kingdom of God with the resources that He's given you—because when you become a kingdom investor, God will "stock" you. He'll bless you with a rich harvest so that He can increase His investments through you.

Remember Isaiah 55:10–11, "For as the rain cometh down, and the snow from heaven, and returneth not thither, but watereth the earth, and maketh it bring forth and bud, that it may give seed to the sower, and bread to the eater: So shall my word be that goeth forth out of my mouth: it shall not return unto me void, but it shall accomplish that which I please, and it shall prosper *in the thing* whereto I sent it."

- 6 -
The "IF" Condition

Believers love to declare the blessings in Deuteronomy 28, "Oh, yes! I'm blessed in the city, blessed in the field, blessed when I go in, and blessed when I come out." Yet we sometimes forget this scripture starts by saying, "And it shall come to pass, if thou shalt hearken diligently unto the voice of the Lord thy God, to observe *and* do all his commandments which I command thee this day..." (v. 1) There's an "IF" condition. IF is a small word, but it has a lot of power. It means the whole matter hinges on that one word.

If you're thinking, *He's using the Old Testament. We're not under that old covenant anymore*, let me remind you of something Jesus said, "If ye abide in me, and my words abide in you, ye shall ask what ye will, and it shall be done unto you" (John 15:7).

One thing I had to learn about building foundations is that God isn't going to build on something that's not solid. Why? He doesn't want to kill you. He knows that the foundation is going to crumble on you. This isn't punishment; *it's mercy*. God knows that if He adds more to where you are right now, it will overwhelm you. Think about it. What have you been trying to build on that you haven't first increased the foundation? When my wife and I decided to build an addition onto our house, we had to break ground and add to the foundation first. We couldn't attach the new addition without adding to the foundation.

The problem with building onto an existing foundation is that part of it has to be torn up and ripped up before you can build up. On a spiritual level, most of us want God to do the changing so that we can stay exactly where we are. We say, "God, just bless me where I am. I'll let *this* go when *that's* here." That's not reality. I had to give up some things to build the addition: I had to lose a driveway and an entrance into my backyard. I had to have piles of dirt thrown all over the place that looked messy and sloppy. Workers had to come in with bulldozers and plow up my blacktop, and then I had to replace the blacktop after they'd finished. I had to sacrifice something in order to get what I was believing for.

Most Christians don't want to do this. We want to hide the issue and say, "Well, God, I'm presenting what You gave me back to You..." without making any investment whatsoever. "Now, increase me," we say, "I've quoted the scriptures and paid my tithes..." We've overlooked the fact that as His children, God requires us to increase in the

Harvest Time: What's That All About?

Spirit before He increases us monetarily. A rich fool is still a fool. Proverbs 21:20 says, "A fool and his money soon part." You can't be truly prosperous and still be a fool in the Spirit! God knows that even though you're claiming *the wealth of the sinner is laid up for the just*, the sinner will be getting it right back from you in ninety days.

I've literally seen this happen. People have gotten big settlements and it was all gone in less than a year. Before the settlement, they'd been living well on eighteen thousand a year. Then after receiving the settlement, they went through fifty thousand dollars in three months. I knew somebody who went through four hundred thousand dollars in less than a year. That was building on no foundation. God gave that individual provision to expand the foundation, but instead, the person tried to go straight up…buying new cars, new houses, new this, new that…new shoes, a pair of sneakers for every day of the week…*up, up, up.*

If you received a windfall blessing, would you build up or build down? Would you build up or build out? Be honest. Do you have a tendency to always build up just to improve your lifestyle, or do you invest and try to create opportunities to grow? Do you keep trying to improve your status in life without adding to your foundation?

Years ago when we were poor, beepers were the big thing—if you had a beeper, you were "living large." And I wanted one. At the time, I was trying to be a businessman so I was trying to find out how to get a beeper, but I couldn't afford one. I could barely keep my phone connected. So I came up with an idea: I went to a beeper company, sat down with them and said, "Look, if I get a lot of beepers from you and set up a business account, how much would you charge me for the beepers?" They gave me a price that was about half of what they would normally charge. I said, "How many beepers do I have to take?" "Fifty." Satisfied, I said, "That sounds great."

I took fifty beepers, made a spreadsheet on my computer to track the sales, and became a beeper distributor. I collected money every month from all of my customers. Though I didn't make a lot of surplus, I made enough to keep my beeper on and have a few dollars in my pocket. I got a free beeper out of the deal and some extra money for carfare. Before long, other beeper companies started calling me to find out if I wanted to sell their product. I told them, "No, I don't want to go into the beeper business." Why? I had a goal and I had reached it. I just wanted a free beeper.

Do you see the principle? Even in my need, I expanded my foundation so that I could reap the benefit. In the meantime, other people

Harvest Principle I: Break Ground for the Harvest

received benefits too. They bought beepers from me cheaper than they could have someplace else. This is how God operates…because He's in the process of building His kingdom—not just your pocketbook.

Let the expansion process begin. Start by getting your priorities in order with God, and then let Him add to your foundation. If you catch His vision and obey what He tells you to do, you will be blessed indeed.

- 7 -

According to Your Faith…

Luke 19 teaches another good lesson, "And another came, saying, Lord, behold, *here* is thy pound, which I have kept laid up in a napkin: for I feared thee, because thou art an austere man: thou takest up that thou layedst not down, and reapest that thou didst not sow" (vv. 20–21). What he was saying in plain language was, "I didn't do anything with the gift that you gave me because you're not a good man and you take stuff that doesn't belong to you."

Obviously, this servant's information was inaccurate—because his two buddies had just received a generous settlement. Perhaps he'd heard rumors or for some reason had a false impression of God. He'd heard some religious doctrine like, "He might not be there when you want Him, but He's right on time," or, "Well, the Lord has to break you before He can make you. He has to take you through the valley before He brings you to the mountaintop." He'd probably heard all of that junk, so he had a picture of the master that was different than the other two servants—because they got blessed and he got whipped.

The other two men said, "Hey, if we work this opportunity, we're going to get blessed!" The fear of the unfaithful man was based on a lie; as a result, he didn't invest the gift that God had given him. Let's look at the outcome, "And he saith unto him, Out of thine own mouth will I judge thee, thou wicked servant…" Watch out! Didn't Jesus say, "According to your faith be it unto you…"? (See Matthew 9:29.) Remember, Jesus was telling this story!

Let's continue, "…Thou knewest that I was an austere man, taking up that I laid not down, and reaping that I did not sow: Wherefore then gavest not thou my money into the bank, that at my coming I might have required mine own with usury?" (vv. 22–23). Here's the translation, "If you think I'm such a bad and mean man, then why didn't you take my money and put it in the bank so I could at least have earned some interest?" Verses 24 and 25 continue, "And he said unto them that stood by, Take from him the pound, and give *it* to him that hath ten pounds. (And they said unto him, Lord, he hath ten pounds.)" That really sounds like church people, doesn't it?

The point is, God wanted to give more to the one who did more. Now, let's keep reading, "For I say unto you, That unto everyone which hath shall be given; and from him that hath not, even that he hath shall be taken away from him" (v. 26). In this passage, the thing that each servant possessed was monetary. However, I also apply it on a more general level.

The Bible promises that your gifts (those God-given abilities that you possess) will bring you before kings (see Proverbs 18:16). If you don't utilize them well, God could use somebody else who has been anointed with similar gifts, and you'd lose your opportunity. Your gifts sustain you. That's why you're able to keep that job, even if you haven't been using your abilities to their fullest potential.

Remember, the nobleman gave each servant start up cash, and each one utilized it according to his own perception. God doesn't play the "Guess which hand?" game, but He does require that you believe. Do you want to live an abundant life and reap the rich harvest God desires for you to have as His covenant son or daughter? Then put your faith in Him and invest what He's given you to help build His kingdom. The more you sow, the more you'll reap...and if you don't sow, you can lose your rewards. It's all according to your faith. Are you ready for the harvest?

Pray and Declare Your Harvest!

Say this out loud, "I believe the blessings of the Lord are clear and precise. The Word promises that God isn't the author of confusion; therefore, if I'm confused, it's not from God. I know that I am one of His sheep and that I can hear His voice. The Lord's direction for my life is sure, and because I'm my Father's child, I'm an investor. I invest strong and my investments are blessed because I'm faithful with what God has given me. I firmly believe that as I obediently and faithfully manage the resources God has given me, He will shower me with greater opportunities to do more for His kingdom. Amen."

HARVEST PRINCIPLE I
SEVEN WAYS TO BREAK GROUND FOR THE HARVEST

Understand True Prosperity
Gen. 1:26, Jn. 14:12, Matt. 6:33

Understand Your True Foundation
Num. 23:19, Lk. 14:28–30

Aspire to Nobility in God's Kingdom
Lk. 19:12–15, Deut. 28:13

Be Willing to Expand
Lk. 19:16–21

Become a Kingdom Investor
Prov. 11:29, Isa. 55:10–11, 1 Cor. 2:9

Learn How to Increase in the Spirit
Deut. 28:1, Jn. 15:7

Believe that God Wants to Prosper You
Lk. 19:20–26, Matt. 9:29

Harvest Principle II

Prepare the Soil

- 8 -
Plowing Comes First

Proverbs 20:4 says, "The sluggard will not plow by reason of the cold; *therefore* shall he beg in harvest, and *have* nothing." The same verse in the Amplified version reads, "The sluggard does not plow when winter sets in; therefore he begs in harvest and has nothing." In other words, the lazy person won't plow.

I had never seen or heard this scripture preached in my life. I'd always heard, "Give and it shall be given unto you...any man that soweth shall reap, pressed down, shaken together, running over . . ." The problem is, as human beings, we have a tendency to bring God down to our level instead of coming up to His. So when God gives us a revelation, we try to relate it to where we are, not to where He's leading us.

As I considered Proverbs 20:4, God gave me a serious revelation. I said, "Father, I know what You're saying, but I'm always giving." He responded, "Read it again." I read it again. "It says *that* man is lazy," I protested, "I'm not lazy." "Read it," He repeated. I read it again.

At the time, I didn't have anything. I was tired of being poor and hungry...so finally, I said to the Lord, "Okay, that sounds like me...but I don't get the lazy part, Lord. I'm a sower. I give." Do you feel this way? Am I speaking to your life right now? Have you ever wondered, *Where are all of the miracles and blessings I hear people talking about...where somebody just walks up and hands them fifty thousand dollars? When is that going to happen to me? I'm always giving. Where are the miracle blessings people are always talking about on television? Do they make this stuff up, or does it really happen?* If so, it's important that you read this story (and this entire book) very carefully.

God urged me, "Read it again, slowly." Reluctantly, I slowed myself down and started again...then I heard God say, "I'll come back to you tomorrow when you're ready to read it." "Okay, okay, okay, God..." I checked my attitude and slowly started again, "The sluggard will not plow by reason of the cold..." Suddenly, it hit me. The verse didn't say, "sow." It said, "plow."

God was trying to teach me a new principle and I kept trying to relate it to where I was...*sowing*. Plowing is not sowing. In spiritual terms, I'd always thought of plowing and sowing together. I'd tell myself, *You must plow, you've got to sow, you've got to give some-*

thing…sow your seed. The principles obviously weren't the same, but I had been operating under the assumption that they were synonymous. Sowing and plowing are as different in the spirit realm as they are in the natural.

Here's the distinction: *You must plow before you sow*. Plowing prepares the ground for sowing. When seeds are sown in ground that's been prepared by thorough plowing, they can produce a strong harvest.

I was startled. Then I came to a realization, *Even though I've heard the word "plow," I don't have a clue what it is*. To be honest, people use words in sentences every day without investigating what they really mean. That's when I went to my wife…she had been raised in the country, so I knew that she could tell me what I needed to know. "Honey, God just showed me something," I said. "This scripture doesn't say a person won't *sow*. It says he won't *plow*. I'm getting a sense that plowing is different than sowing." She said, "Oh, yes…" and started breaking down the principles. I realized why a lot of believers don't get a breakthrough, even if they're sowing. They haven't plowed. They haven't prepared the soil.

- 9 -

What is Plowing?

Plowing is dirt cleaning. On the spiritual side, we have to remember that we were made from the dirt. Sometimes other elements get mixed in with our "dirt" and keep us from reaping a fruitful harvest, even if we're great givers. That's where I was during that season of my life, so God really began to deal with me. He started by giving me this word of correction, "Stop saying that I'm allowing you to lack what you need in order to teach you something." In other words, God instructs us through the counsel of His Word—not by making us suffer. So when He corrected my faulty thinking, I had to face the fact that my own mistakes were causing me to suffer—not God.

Truthfully, if you want to use the "suffering doctrine" as an excuse for your financial woes, ultimately you'd still have to reach a conclusion. If two, three, or four years pass and you're still experiencing the same difficulties in the area of finances, either God's a bad teacher or you're a stupid student. Don't keep blaming your plowing problem on God. He's trying to get you to clean your dirt. Spiritually speaking, God's waiting for you to begin dealing with the issues that are in your heart. Your soil needs to be purified.

If you are harboring unforgiveness or bitterness, God wants you to deal with it. If there's larceny in your heart, then you need to get it right before God. What is larceny? It's a spirit that is going largely unchecked in the body of Christ. It blows my mind that a Christian would walk into a store, open a bag of cookies, eat the whole bag, and then leave it in the cart while paying for the rest of the items. The same would be true if a believer were to pick up a bundle of grapes and eat most of them before they're actually weighed during check-out.

You might be thinking, *Come on, Pastor, let's get to the deep stuff.* This is the deep stuff! The Word says that the "little foxes" spoil the vines (see Song of Songs 2:15). Little foxes are extremely dangerous. If a bear attacks your vines, it's obvious to everybody. In other words, if you come to church drunk, people can easily see that...but little foxes eat at the roots. To the common eye, the vines still look like they're flourishing while the foxes are having a feast. You're still declaring, "Hallelujah! I'm blessed and highly favored of the Lord! If God be with me, who can be against me?" You're still looking good, and you're still saying the right things; but deep down, you're dying slowly.

That's why I never promote people based on their charisma. I watch them long enough to see their character—long enough to look down and see their roots. I want to be sure that a person's roots are still connected and healthy. A car could be speeding down the road at one hundred miles per hour when the motor dies. If you're standing down the road from the car when it happens, it still looks like it's zooming toward you; but in reality, it's in the process of coming to a complete stop.

God is very clear about *little foxes*. First Samuel 15:22 says, "...Hath the Lord *as great* delight in burnt offerings and sacrifices, as in obeying the voice of the Lord? Behold, to obey *is* better than sacrifice, *and* to hearken than the fat of rams." God doesn't care about the image you present to others so that they will say you're a good sister or brother in the Lord. He's concerned with the "little things" that nobody sees except Him and you; the hidden things that would cause Him to say, "Because you did this in private, I'm going to promote you openly."

Remember Cain and Abel. Cain brought an offering that was not pleasing to God. This can happen today when you sacrifice the thing that you think God wants, but it's not what He asked you for. This type of offering then becomes your alternative to obedience—and God doesn't accept "alternative offerings." He only values what you give in obedience to His Word. Don't be like Cain. Don't bring what you have presumed to be an acceptable offering to the Lord, and then when He doesn't bless it, let the *little foxes* in your heart deceive you until you lose your inheritance. (See Genesis 4:1–16.)

Let me close with this. According to Proverbs 22:1, a good name is to be desired over wealth and riches, and favor rather than silver and gold. This means we need to start plowing; we need to go to the roots and deal with the "little foxes" that can spoil the vines and hinder our harvest. Come clean and give God the obedience that He desires, not the sacrifices you think He should have. God wants obedience.

- 10 -

The Principles of Plowing

When I asked my wife to explain the principle of plowing to me in detail, she took a deep breath as if old memories were flashing through her mind and said, "Honey, plowing is harder than sowing." I was more ready than ever to hear what she had to say. God had opened my spirit through the scriptures that my family was poor, not because I wasn't sowing, but because I wasn't plowing.

Angela continued, "Let me tell you what happens. You have to put on a big hat because it's hot in the sun. Then you get down on your hands and knees, find weeds, and rip them up. You have to get all of the impurities, rocks, and dead stuff out of the soil that would make it unfertile. Then you have to turn the ground over, flip it again, and put fertilizer down to make the soil potent." Back when my wife had to plow, they didn't have cute little fertilizer crystals; they used the real stuff. Manure. The manure was dry, so they had to stick their hands in it, crumble it up, sprinkle it on the ground, and mix it into the soil. Afterwards, they'd let the ground sit so that it would be ready to receive a seed. There was a lot of work involved.

As I listened, I thought to myself, *I haven't been plowing*. In simple terms, plowing gets the ground ready to support a good harvest. You can sow a seed in ground that hasn't been plowed or fertilized and crops will spring up—but not to their maximum yield. That's why so many Christians aren't reaping God's best. They're blessed…they have jobs, God is meeting their needs, and they're paying their bills. When they need an increase, it shows up. But they're still not seeing that abundant "breakthrough harvest" because the ground of their hearts wasn't prepared before they sowed a seed.

Harvest Time: What's That All About?

Let me summarize a parable that Jesus taught in Matthew 13:3–9 and 18–23. A man sowed seed on three different types of soil: stony ground, thorny ground, and good ground. The good ground brought forth a harvest yielding thirty, sixty, or one hundredfold. Again, the ground represents your heart. So the process of cleaning the ground doesn't mean that you clean up your behavior in church, or dress up in nice clothes—it means that you have some old, dead stuff inside of you that isn't right before God, and it has to be cleaned out by the Word. Afterwards, your heart must be fertilized...then you'll be able to sow your seeds and reap a good harvest.

What about people who don't know Jesus? How are they able to prosper financially? God has established this principle in the universe: When you sow, you reap. Then when you become a child of God, you are covered under His covenant. This means when the enemy comes, he should find no wickedness in you. Prosperity touches much more than finances. According to God's covenant, it covers every area of your life: spiritual, emotional, financial, and so on. People can make a lot of money, but that doesn't mean they're prosperous.

Jesus said in Matthew 5:23–24, "Therefore, if thou bring thy gift to the altar, and there rememberest that thy brother hath ought against thee; leave there thy gift before the altar, and go thy way; first be reconciled to thy brother, and then come and offer thy gift." This is an example of plowing. It's a spiritual illustration that shows one example of how to clean and fertilize the soil before you come back to God to plant your seed. You can plant your seed without plowing, but again, it's not going to yield a maximum harvest.

At that moment, I realized that I owed some apologies...I needed to get things right and make amends with some people. I had been harboring thoughts and opinions in my heart about situations that had happened in the past, and I had talked about them even when I felt a little cramp of conviction in my spirit.

God said to me, "Listen. Here's the problem with believers that don't understand this principle. If I convict them in an area and they resist, I'll convict them again. When they resist again, they don't feel the conviction as strongly." After God convicts you four or five times about something and you keep resisting, He'll withdraw that conviction. Then you'll come to the conclusion that He's letting you have what you want. In reality, He's simply stepping back and letting you reap what you've decided to reap. He's really saying, "Okay, you're determined to reap judgment, so I'm going to step back and let you reap it."

Is this hitting home? Plain and simple, there are things we do that can stop the process of prosperity in our lives. We'll be seeking God and saying, "Lord, I need to pay my mortgage…" and He'll respond, "Yes, baby. I want you to pay that mortgage. I put that house on your heart…" or, "I gave you the desire for that business." In this, God is saying, "You didn't think this stuff up; I put these desires inside of you…but now, you want to hold My hand and lead Me in how you want to be blessed. I know how to bless you better than you even know what blessing is."

Then God will begin to deal with you about something that you think is so stupid and minute, and you'll say, "Yes, Lord…I know." Beware of this attitude. If you have to feel like you know everything, even when you're being corrected, check yourself. When I'm counseling a person and he or she constantly tries to match me scripture for scripture, it's a sure sign that the "ground" needs some work. Some plowing needs to be done; otherwise, reaping will be minimal.

- 11 -
Start at Ground Zero

The cleaning process is the most important part of the reaping process. I remember when folks used to say, "You'd better get your house in order before the Lord comes." This refers to the cleaning process. The man in Proverbs 20:4 wouldn't "clean his house," so when harvest time came, he didn't get an answer to his prayer…and he was crying and begging because he didn't have any food. Do you know anyone like that? He or she will say, "I've prayed and prayed. I've sought the Lord. I gave my tithe, went to church every Sunday…and God's never answered my prayer." This person didn't take the time before God to get his or her heart clean.

Too many people still have rocks, weeds, and impurities in the ground of their hearts, so they're either sowing and not reaping at all, or they're reaping a minimal harvest. The dirt must be purified and fertilized. Genesis 2:7 says, "And the LORD God formed man *of* the dust of the ground, and breathed into his nostrils the breath of life; and man became a living soul." For a full year, God had me dealing with plowing issues from the pulpit: coming clean and confessing our sins before God, being real with each other, not trying to present a "Christian image" when we know that unforgiveness, hatred, and bitterness are in our hearts, and so on. Then He allowed me to begin teaching *Harvest Time*.

Jesus told us to pray after this manner, "...Our Father which are in heaven, Hallowed be thy name. Thy kingdom come. Thy will be done in earth, as *it is* in heaven" (Matthew 6:9–10). No matter how we may try to cover it up, God knows our dirt. He formed us from its substance. He knows what's in our hearts...that's why I teach that we must pray for His will to be done in the "earth" of our hearts—not just the physical earth in which we live. King David acknowledged this when he prayed, "Behold, thou desirest truth in the inward parts: and in the hidden *part* thou shalt make me to know wisdom" (Psalm 51:6).

It used to puzzle me that God called David *a man after His own heart*. David had committed murder, and he was a liar and an adulterer. How could God see him this way? Then I began to study about David's life, and I saw that he was a repentant man. Whenever his sin was exposed, he didn't try to place the blame on somebody else, or say that God made him do it. He'd confess, "I've sinned before you, God." Then he'd break down and cry. David had a contrite heart. That's the "good soil" God is looking for.

God doesn't expect you to be perfect; He wants your heart to be pure and real so that you can receive everything He has for you. This takes some plowing: owning up to what's really in your heart, bringing it before God, and then being obedient to correct it. If you don't confess your faults and plow up that unfertile ground, your harvest is going to be stagnated or stopped.

Whatever it is, admit it. Be willing to say, "I really haven't forgiven this person like I said I did," or, "I really don't walk in love toward that person like I should"—whatever is necessary to keep your heart pure before God. Accept the fact that there's sin in your life. Deal with it instead of hiding it and trying to pretend that it doesn't exist. *It's there*. So put your hand to the plow. Get your spiritual house in order. God made you from the dirt, so He is more than equipped to help you get through the plowing process.

- 12 -
Plow Patiently

Another thing we can learn from King David is not to promote ourselves before God promotes us. Pride will kill a harvest. Paul said in Romans 12:3, "For I say, through the grace given unto me, to every man that is among you, not to think *of himself* more highly than he ought to think; but to think soberly, according as God hath dealt to every man the measure of faith." Self-promotion is dangerous.

For example, I'm not able to preach because I have a lot of head knowledge about scripture…I can preach because God has given me an anointing to be a pastor and teacher. By His grace, that's who I am. If you know more scripture than I do and try to get in the pulpit without being anointed by God, get ready for a fall. You might as well stand up in front of the church and say, "Wa, wa, wa, wa…" because that's all your sermon will mean to anybody. You may be able to open a book of the Bible, discern which day of the week Paul wrote it, how he was feeling at the time, and what he ate for breakfast—but the end result is, if God hasn't anointed you to deliver His Word, you won't have enough anointing to blow out a match.

Proverbs 16:18–19 says, "Pride *goeth* before destruction, and an haughty spirit before a fall. Better *it is to be* of an humble spirit with the lowly, than to divide the spoil with the proud." It's very common for believers to feel like we've arrived, and I believe it all boils down to impatience. Too often, we try to put ourselves in places where God hasn't promoted and appointed us. We try to take ground that God hasn't given us. Instead, we should be sober about God's plowing process. As God deals with the impurities in our "soil," we must learn how to let His work be completed in us.

Jesus said that when you're invited to a banquet you shouldn't sit at the head of the table, because someone greater than you will come. If you are asked to take another seat, you'll look like a big idiot. (See Luke 14:8–10.) This happens to some people all the time and they still don't learn. Impatient in the things of God, they still try to push their way to the head of the table. The Bible clearly tells us to take the lesser seat. Then if the host recognizes you, he'll bring you to that place of honor.

Listen closely to what I'm saying. When a person always seeks promotion, but never seeks the anointing, there's a serious issue. People naturally want to equate promotion with anointing, but they definitely are not the same.

Consider the life of Moses. He was born an Israelite, yet according to the plan and grace of God, he ended up being raised in the house of a king—which enabled him to be well trained on how to be a leader in the world's system. When Moses became a man he began to realize, "I'm not an Egyptian. I'm an Israelite, and since I've been raised in a royal house, I'm going to use the techniques I've learned to take leadership." Moses saw an Egyptian soldier whipping an Israelite, and when he intervened he killed that soldier, because that's what he knew. *That's self-promotion.* Later, Moses saw two Hebrew men arguing, ran over to them and said, "Can't we all just get along?" (I'm paraphrasing, of course.) They turned to him and said, "What's it to you? Are you going to kill us, too?" Caught in his sin, Moses fled to the desert. He had become a wanted criminal. (See Exodus 2:1–15.)

When you promote yourself, you usually end up operating in one of two spirits. First, you become a murderer by always judging and criticizing everybody else. "I don't see why she's there...I should be doing that...I've been here longer than she has." These words reveal a murderous spirit. You start destroying everybody else's gifts because you want yours to be promoted *right now*.

Second, when you seek to promote yourself too soon you can become a busybody. Busybodies never mind their own business. They try to solve everybody else's problems, but all the while, fail to straighten out their own house. Busybodies want to tell people how to raise their kids, but they can't get their own kids to live right. It applies in every area.

Proverbs 14:4 says, "Where no oxen are, the grain crib is empty, but much increase [of crops] comes by the strength of the ox" (Ampl.). Here's what I gleaned from this scripture. If you want the power of the ox, you have to deal with the mess in the stall. If you want POWER, God says you'd better be ready to clean up the mess. Remember, we're talking about plowing to reap a greater harvest. In order for God to promote you, you have to be willing to humble yourself so that He can raise you up in due season.

You can sow all of the seed you want, but if you refuse to plow because it's cold...according to Proverbs 20:4...you'll be begging during harvest time. If you'll be patient during the plowing process, God will appoint you to a place of power when harvest time comes—because His anointing will rest upon you. Remember, what God doesn't appoint, He doesn't anoint.

- 13 -

The Three C's

If you really want to prosper in the things of God, then you need to learn the *Three C's*. **First, you need to have an understanding of covenant.** I'm not talking about simply taking communion, because some people take communion from the wrong motivation and with an unplowed heart. Never try to use the covenant of God to get what you want. Don't play with God like that. It's extremely dangerous. Too many people even bring their tithes and offerings with the wrong motivation. Our covenant relationship with God must be the basis of everything we do for Him.

Covenant living isn't something God instituted to help you out of trouble; covenant is something that you live by all the time. It's a daily lifestyle, not something you do when your back's against the wall. Covenant is an instant exchange between you and God when you can say, "Everything I have belongs to You, and everything You have belongs to me." This means if everything God has doesn't belong to you right now, then everything you have doesn't yet belong to Him.

Bear with me. I'm not trying to beat you up; I'm trying to help you get through the plowing process. At the same time, I want to stop the devil from jerking you around with those "little foxes" that have been spoiling your vines.

We're taking a practical, step-by-step approach to the process of sowing and reaping. Why? I had been in church for years. I had learned how to sow, but nobody taught me how to reap. I knew about, "Give and it will be given unto you..." and I was giving—yet we barely had enough to pay our bills. I often wondered, *When is it going to be given unto me...good measure, pressed down, shaken together...?*

That's why you must embrace the entire process. It is also why the first thing you must understand is your covenant relationship with God. When everything you have in every aspect of your life is available to God in every way, I promise you that every aspect of God's deity will be available to you. I've heard people say, "Jesus was a poor man." A poor man couldn't take two fish and five loaves of bread and feed twenty thousand people! A covenant believer might not have a lot of money in the bank, but he or she knows how to reach up into heaven and pull down something when it's needed. That's the true definition of being rich. Even if you don't have hundreds of thousands in the bank, you're still able to get your hands on what you need when you need it.

Some people say, "But Pastor, I have to consecrate myself." Live a consecrated life! Don't just consecrate when you need something. Don't treat God like Exlax. Keep your soil clean. Don't try to cram for blessings by fasting for seven days...live a fasted life. Turn off the programs you've been watching on television that are no good for your spirit. Stop having conversations that prick your heart. When you say something that grieves the Holy Spirit, stop and repent. Obey Him instantly.

Be a person of covenant. Be available to God twenty-four hours a day, seven days a week, and He'll be available to you the same way. God shouldn't have to bring you through a process of sending three angels, crashing lightening across your room, and shaking your room with violent earthquakes to get you to obey His Spirit.

Don't get me wrong. By stressing the plowing process, I'm not against the teaching that *money* can *cometh*. But I do know this: If you claim *money cometh*, it will come. Then immediately Satan will cometh to take the seed. So if you're not right in spirit, *money will cometh, satan will cometh, and then money will goeth as fast as it has cometh.*

I've witnessed people being blessed financially and then a month later they can't show you where that blessing is. When it came, the whole church was jumping around, screaming and rejoicing—and then three weeks later they're back to the way they were before the blessing came. When you ask what happened, they say, "Well, just pray for me." It's a shame that many praise reports and testimonies from God's people are only as big as their last breakthrough. It grieves me when somebody wants to stand in front of the church and get everybody excited about something they're only going to keep for three weeks. That's a temporary breakthrough, and that doesn't sound like my God.

John 8:36 says, "So if the Son liberates you [makes you free men], then you are really {and} unquestionably free" (Ampl.). Does this mean you stay free for a little while? No! Covenant is for keeps…that is, *if you keep it.*

The second "C" is change. This means we have to be a people of repentance, just like King David. Unfortunately, we don't tend to use this word correctly. We use it to say, "I'm sorry for what I did until I do it again." That's not repentance. Repentance isn't saying, "I'm sorry, God, that I did what I did…" and then you let your male friend come over again at bedtime. Repentance means that you make a total turn-around and head in the opposite direction…that way, you don't keep doing it again, and again, and again. (See Romans 6:1–6.) If you're one of those people that says, "Well, it's a struggle, Pastor," then face it. You haven't repented.

When Pharaoh's wife tempted Joseph, he ran out of that place! (See Genesis 39:7–12.) So if you've truly repented, take back your keys, give back his toothbrush and change of underwear, and say, "I don't care how late it gets, you can't stay in my house." That's repentance. "I'm working on it..." isn't repentance. Lay your sin down at the altar and leave it there. Don't work on it. Let God cleanse the impurities out of your soil. Embrace your covenant relationship with your heavenly Father and repent. He'll give you the strength to change.

Let me add a little something about "good ground." It is always stronger for the next year's crop. As the soil of your heart changes, you can expect the next harvest to be bigger than the first. This is exponential increase...yielding increasingly greater harvests as you grow in God.

The third "C" is commitment to the truth, regardless of the cost. This is vitally important because most Christians that I've met know the Word is true, until it puts them in a corner and they have to stand. Are you committed to the truth when you say, "The Lord shall supply all my needs, Pastor," and then you turn around and lie on your tax return to get a few extra dollars? What about keeping your word? "Well, Pastor, I promised to give these dresses to this sister because I was expecting a check to come, but it didn't." If you don't keep your word, you're not committed to the truth.

Psalm 15:4 exhorts us to swear to our own hurt and change not. If you give your word to somebody, be where you said you're going to be and do what you said you would do...even if it costs you more than you expected. God will repay it. Just stand by your word. Don't try to find another scripture and quote it to God in order to weasel your way out of something; you can't outsmart God! He's already established laws in the spirit realm so that when you do something wrong a correction comes to your spirit. At that point, you must embrace the truth and submit to the correction.

By learning the Three C's, you'll be able to plow more efficiently. And as a result...you'll reap a rich harvest.

- 14 -

Put Your Hands to the Plow

It's time to prepare the soil of your heart for a rich harvest, so don't let anything stop you from plowing. When God starts speaking a word of correction to your spirit, He usually starts by speaking it *to* you *through* you. If you're listening to His voice in prayer and through the Word, you'll get a check in your spirit when it's time to plow. Obey...immediately. Turn off that television show when something inside of you says, "You don't need to be watching this." Respond to the little cold chill that hits your spirit when somebody calls you and starts to gossip. Don't say, "I shouldn't be listening to this, but I just want to know what's going on so I can pray." Learn to submit under a corrective word of obedience.

James 2:10–11 says, "For whosoever shall keep the whole law, and yet offend in one *point,* he is guilty of all. For he that said, Do not commit adultery, said also, Do not kill. Now if thou commit no adultery, yet if thou kill, thou art become a transgressor of the law." The consequences of sin are exactly the same regardless of what you do. It might be easy for you to say that you'd never commit murder. You could also find it easy to say, "I can't believe that person sold drugs." Yet, while you're talking about him, you're reaping the same judgment that he's reaping for drug dealing! We rationalize our own sins by saying, "At least I don't do *that*..."

When this happens, you've taken the rule of balance from God and given it to yourself. You've decided that you have the right to judge the scale of what's right and what's wrong in His eyes, and God can't be pleased with that. (See Proverbs 11:1.) What's actually taking place is this: God made you in His image and then you turned around and returned the favor by recreating God in your image. So much of what we're doing in the body of Christ—and calling it God—isn't really God at all. It's only a facsimile of Him.

When you get a check in your spirit from the Holy Ghost, stop and take what I call a "spiritual picture." Capture what you're feeling at that moment and then remember what you felt before you found yourself in that last trial. For example, every time you got with that wrong man or woman, that same feeling came up in your spirit. You might be saying, "He's not like the other guy...", yet you're still getting that same feeling. Don't keep pushing through and silence the voice in your spirit because you want what you want. Let God plow through the soil of your heart.

You might be saying, "I'm believing God for a million dollars," but God is saying, "No, no, no...I want you to pray that you'll learn how to clean up this house I've given you." If you silence that voice, you'll end up wondering why you couldn't get that new place you've desired for three years. Then you'll rationalize, "It's in God's timing." No! When God speaks something to you, that is His timing. When He gives you a sense of something, it's simply that.

Harvest Principle II: Prepare the Soil

For example, you may have a divine sense that at some point in your life you'll be going into the ministry. That will come in "due season." On the other hand, when God reveals a "now" word to you, or a prophet comes and speaks a word that it's your season, God means for it to happen NOW. He doesn't mean for it to happen years later. When God releases a "now" word, He's ready for it to take place. That means if there's a hold up, it's on you, not God. When you fail to discern a "now season," you can miss your blessings. So get the container of your spirit ready now. The longer you take to obey after receiving a "now" word from God, the longer it will take for the word to come to pass. Plowing must be done.

For example, you might fall on your face and say, "Lord, I don't understand why I'm going through this." And He'll say, "Your cousin, Susan…" "Okay…I know that. I'm going to get to that God." Only this wasn't the first time He told you; He said it two years ago. But you're still saying, "I'm going to call her…but Lord, could You just show me anything else that I'm doing wrong?" And He keeps saying, "Your cousin, Susan…" Put your hand to the plow! Don't say, "Yeah, yeah. I haven't spoken to her in five years…but, Lord." After a while, God will stop. He may come back when you're ready to be plowed, or He may step back and let you reap judgment.

Through applying the process of plowing, my family went from total poverty into the total wealth of God. If you obey His Spirit when He calls you to plow, then according to James 4:8–10, He'll do the same for you.

Harvest Time: What's That All About?

Harvest Principle II: Prepare the Soil

Pray and Declare Your Harvest!

Reach your hands up to the heavens and pray with me. Follow me, using your own words, because you know that nagging thing you've been ignoring. You know that person you need to forgive, or the one you need to stop talking to *or* about. You remember that time when you went to the store, picked up some grapes, and ate most of them before you got to the cashier. You know the little foxes.

When you're in a plowing season, God really starts dealing with these things. In doing so, He's saying, "I need to get the spirit of larceny out of you before I can bless you, because if you're used to receiving through conning and stealing, then you don't know how to receive through the laws of prosperity. It doesn't work both ways. Bitter water and sweet water can't come out of the same fountain."

Let's pray. "Father God, search my heart right now. See if there's anything unpleasing in me...even the little things that don't seem to matter. Search out and reveal every aspect of who I am. Help me to search my spirit by Your Spirit, and if there's anything that is unpleasing to You, expose it. If I'm greedy, self-righteous, or am not pleasing You in any way, reveal it to me, Lord. Show me the thing that I've wanted to shut out when You were bringing it to my heart—the thing that has hindered my growth and kept me from moving forward into greatness.

"Right now, Father God, I lay my heart on Your altar. If there's anything in me, anything that brings You pain, please forgive me. Give me the wisdom, grace, and strength to walk it through knowing that You won't make me look foolish in front of anybody, because Your Word promises that '...hope maketh not ashamed...' and Your love has been shed abroad in my heart.

"I desire to be real, God, so I'm taking off the mask. I'm going to stop playing church games. Father God, search me now. Show me everything that I once thought was insignificant that is hindering my walk with You. Help me to clean my spiritual house so the soil of my heart will be ready and the seeds that I sow will bring a fruitful return.

"Purify me, Lord. In Jesus' name, let Your Word begin to do a cleansing work that will never be hindered or stopped. Thank You for preparing my heart to reap a great harvest in Your kingdom. Amen."

HARVEST PRINCIPLE II
SEVEN WAYS TO PREPARE THE SOIL

Understand the Difference between Sowing and Plowing
Prov. 20:4

Understand Why You Need to Plow
Song of Songs 2:15, 1 Sam. 15:22, Prov. 22:1

Let the Plowing Process Begin
Matt. 13:3–9 and 18–23, Matt. 5:23–24

Start at Ground Zero
Gen. 2:7, Ps. 51:6, Matt. 6:9–10

Be Patient as You Plow
Prov. 14:4, 20:4

Embrace the "Three C's"
Rom. 6:1–6, Jn. 8:36, Ps. 15:4

Don't Stop Plowing
Prov. 11:1, Jms. 4:8–10, Prov. 11:5–6

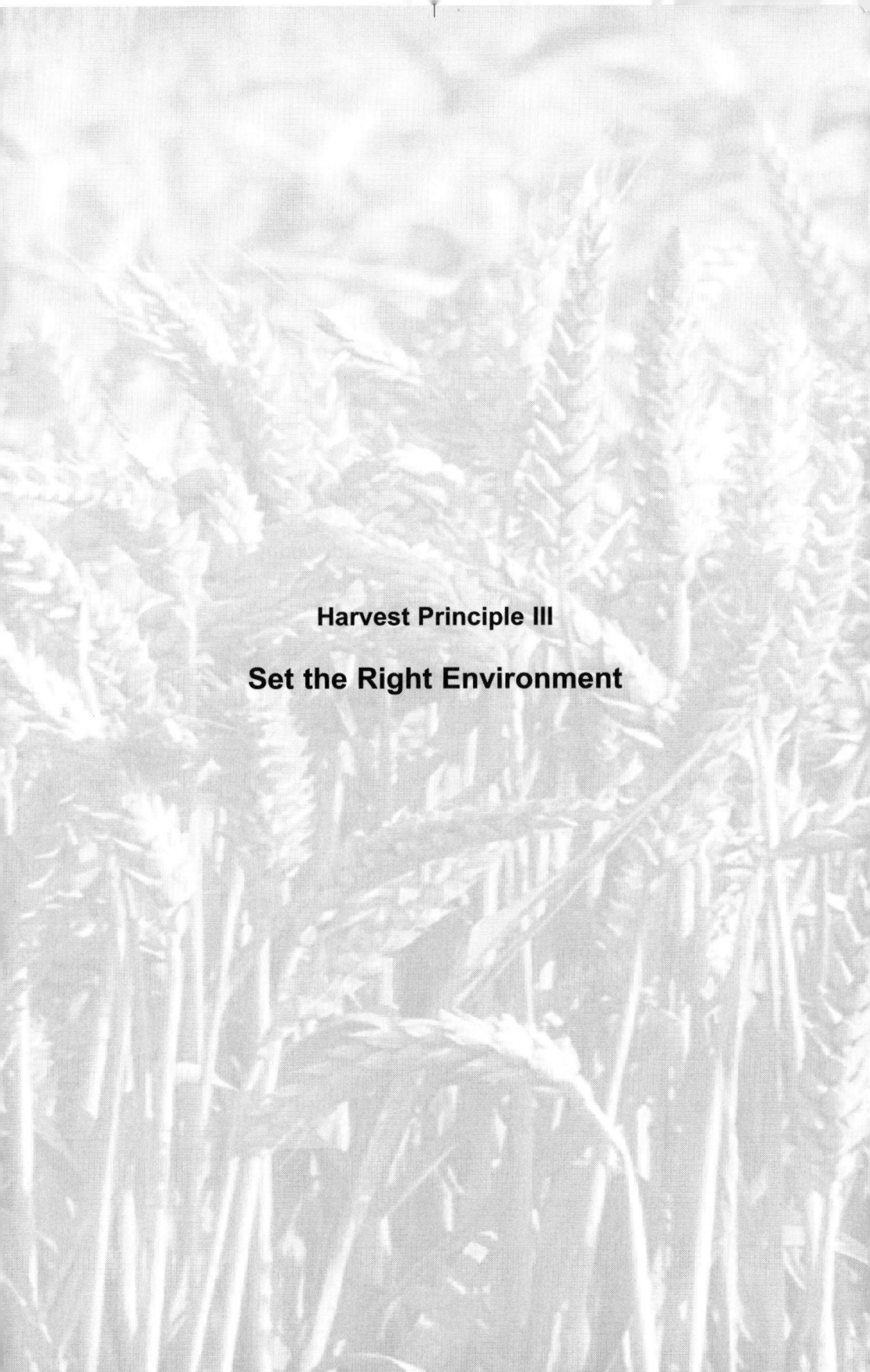

Harvest Principle III

Set the Right Environment

- 15 -
An Open Heaven

Let me start by saying that tithing is not sowing. Malachi 3 says, "Will a man rob God? Yet ye have robbed me. But ye say, Wherein have we robbed thee?....Bring ye all the tithes into the storehouse, that there may be meat in mine house, and prove me now herewith, saith the LORD of hosts, if I will not open you the windows of heaven, and pour you out a blessing, that *there shall* not *be room* enough *to receive it*. And I will rebuke the devourer for your sakes, and he shall not destroy the fruits of your ground; neither shall your vine cast her fruit before the time in the field, saith the LORD of hosts" (vv. 8–12).

Your tithe makes the heavens open up and pour rain down upon the seeds you will sow. Think of it this way: The Bible says that God causes the sun to shine and the rain to come upon the just and the unjust equally (see Matthew 5:45). Considering this in light of Malachi 3, being obedient in giving brings several advantages.

First, the tithe guarantees rain and sunshine at the *right time*. The person who doesn't tithe doesn't know if he's going to get a tornado or a flood. He doesn't have any idea what's going to happen in his harvest field. I pay my tithes, so I am guaranteed that the windows of heaven will open over my field and nourish my seeds right when they need it. Second, giving offerings guarantees crop protection. In practical terms this means because I give offerings, I don't have to shout at or rebuke the devil.

When you bring your tithes *and* offerings, God rebukes the devil for you. That way, you can spend more time praising God and less time marching around declaring, "I bind you, devil; I rebuke you; I cast you out; I come against you." If you're not paying your tithes and offerings, shut up! How can you rebuke the devil when he has keys to your home that you've freely given to him?

When you're doing what God has told you to do, you have automatic authority over the devil. James 4:7 says, "Submit yourself therefore to God. Resist the devil, and he will flee from you." God showed me something about this. He said, "The devil is standing there, watching people scream at him, 'I rebuke you; get out of my house; I command you; let my husband go; let my children go...' and he's saying, 'So that's how you're going to act in front of your Christian friends. Wait until I get you home and see what I do to you.'" (Smile.) Isn't this what you do with your kids? "Oh, so you want to act up and embarrass me out here? Wait until I get you home..."

Satan knows if you've been striking a little contract under the table by withholding your tithes and offerings. Watch out! The next time you have to start binding the devil, make sure that you're submitted to God. I've had people come to me and say, "Pastor, we prayed after you spoke that word and the devil came after us harder than before." Maybe he felt like he had rights. God's Word is true. It works all the time. So if His principles don't seem to be working, check your records to see if you've cut any side deals.

The final stage of crop protection has to do with your storehouse. When you put your tithes and offerings in the right place, God will protect your harvest. Let me say this plainly. Your storehouse is the "house" from which God feeds your spirit. You should tithe where the Lord tells you to tithe, and give offerings as the Lord leads you.

Tithing is God's ultimate protection plan. That's why I know if the devil tries to run a game on my finances, he's going to have to deal with God. I don't have to say, "Satan, I bind you off of my finances…I command you to turn them loose in the name of Jesus." You can do the same. Just pay your tithes and the seeds you plant will be blessed and protected. And when you go before the Lord, you can stand on the ground of putting Him in remembrance of His Word.

- 16 -

An Open Heart

Tithing is your reasonable service. Sowing is what you give above the tithe. Both are to be done with an open heart. Second Corinthians 9:7 says, "Every man according as he purposeth in his heart, *so let him give*; not grudgingly, or of necessity: for God loveth a cheerful giver."

People have said to me, "Pastor, I've heard that you're supposed to tithe on the gross, and I've also heard that you're supposed to tithe on the net. Which one should I do?" My answer to them is, "*Neither one*, because the attitude of your heart is wrong. Keep all of it, because the outcome is going to be the same. Your heart isn't in the right posture."

If you have to go through this analysis before deciding to give, are you a cheerful giver? A person with a heart for God believes that in giving, "…it shall be given." With this understanding, we should want to give in God's favor. We won't try to round off God's tithes to our benefit.

Harvest Time: What's That All About?

I always give on the gross, and I don't stop there; I've always done over ten percent. In fact, God had to stop me from giving because I was beginning to give my necessities away. I'd sow money that I needed to pay my rent, saying, "I'm trusting You, Lord..." God would say, "Okay, son, slow down." You can know that you're in the right place to receive a harvest when you're giving so much that God has to tell you to stop, instead of always trying to nudge you to make you give. It is a stench in the nostrils of God for a thief to stand in front of Him saying, "I claim this; I receive that; this is mine..."

Let me say it again: Anything above the tithe is what you sow—*that's your seed*. Some people get it backwards. They say, "I know, Pastor, but I was just believing the Lord, so I took my tithe money and bought that tape series because I wanted to sow that revelation into my life." No, you're a thief. Don't ever use God's money to buy things for yourself.

Get your heart right with God and you'll be able to do what is *reasonable* in His kingdom. When you open your heart in giving, you'll reap a mighty harvest.

- 17 -

A Covenant Relationship

We can't play games with God. Malachi 3:8 says, "...In what way do we rob *or* defraud You? [You have withheld your] tithes and offerings" (Ampl.). You might be thinking, *Wait a minute, how can I withhold an offering?* Remember, you're in a covenant relationship with your Father. Therefore, everything you have should be prepared as an offering. This doesn't mean that you have to give everything you own—but it does mean that everything you have should be available to God if He asks for it.

Remember, covenant means you make all that you have available to God and God makes everything He has available to you. Of course, this is based on the fact that God gave to us first (see John 3:16), which equips us with a new nature to give supernaturally. God gave with all of His heart, so He's only going to trust you with the level of your heart that is open to Him. For example, people have said to me, "Well, Pastor, I don't make a lot of money and I'm really having trouble making ends meet. But I sow my time. You know, I come to church...I help." That's good. When you need time, God will make sure you have all of the time you need—but you're still not going to have any money!

In the book of Genesis, God said, "...Let the earth put forth [tender] vegetation: plants yielding seed and fruit trees yielding fruit whose seed is in itself, each according to its kind, upon the earth. And it was so" (1:11, Ampl.). In light of this, if you say, "I'll go to the nursing home every week...that's my gift to the Lord," that's fine. When you get old and you're in a nursing home, somebody will be there for you. I'm not saying this to be mean or rough; I'm just trying to help.

I come from a computer networking background, so when people come to us for help the first thing I do is troubleshoot. If somebody says, "Pastor, I can't pay my rent," my first question is, "Are you tithing?" Here's why. If I see oranges on a tree, then I know that somebody planted an orange seed. A tree bears fruit after its kind.

Now, let's go back to Malachi 3. God said, "You are cursed with a curse, for you are robbing Me, even this whole nation. Bring all the tithes (the whole tenth of your income) into the storehouse, that there may be food in My house, and prove Me now by it, says the Lord of hosts, if I will not open the windows of heaven for you and pour you out a blessing, that there shall not be room enough to receive it" (vv. 9–10, Ampl.). When God said, "prove Me," that was a powerful statement. Let me tell you why.

When Satan took Jesus up on a mountain in Matthew 4 and said, "If You are the Son of God, throw Yourself down..." Jesus said, "...You shall not tempt, test thoroughly, *or* try exceedingly the Lord your God" (vv. 6–7, Ampl.). Yet, God told us to prove Him in the area of finances. He gave us permission to do so. It's like God was saying, "Put your back against the wall for Me and I'll put My back against the wall for you."

Harvest Time: What's That All About?

Harvest Principle III: Set the Right Environment

Pray and Declare Your Harvest!

Lift your voice to the Lord in prayer. "Father God, I surrender every area of my life to You. I surrender my heart, I surrender my mind…and I surrender my finances. I know that the tithe is Yours, and because I am living in covenant with You, I will obey You and bring my tithes into the storehouse. It is my reasonable service as a child of Your kingdom. I am not a robber. I am a cheerful giver. I will not withhold my tithes and offerings.

"Father, I thank You that as I obey You in the area of my finances, You will open the windows of heaven over my life and pour out rich supernatural blessings. I thank You for rebuking the enemy on my behalf and for protecting my harvest as I give. Father, I thank You that Your Word is true and that my life will be richly blessed as I prove You in this area. Thank You for instructing my spirit and for equipping me to obey You completely. Amen."

Harvest Principle III
Three Ways to Set the Right Environment

Tithe for an Open Heaven
Mal. 3:8–12, Jms. 4:7

Give with an Open Heart
2 Cor. 9:7

Give from a Covenant Relationship with God
Jn. 3:16, Matt. 4:6–7

Harvest Principle IV

Understand the Sowing Process

- 18 -
Sowing is an Investment

God wants to get us to the point that we see our seeds as investments, not simply as "offerings" (in the sense that we give as though we're doing God a favor). Matthew 13:44 says, "The kingdom of heaven is like something precious buried in a field, which a man found and hid again; then in his joy he goes and sells all he has and buys that field."

Honestly, most of my life the word *offering* meant it was time for the Pastor to beg. In some churches, if the offering plate doesn't come back full the first time during an offering, people know they'd better get ready—because it's going to come around three or four more times before it's all said and done.

Different pastors have used different techniques to bring in offerings. Some keep hammering at you..."You're robbing God; you're going to be cursed if you don't give." While this is what the Bible teaches, some have used this scripture in an unscriptural way. I call it the condemnation route. Others have held up pictures of poor orphans in China to motivate people in giving. Men and women of God have used a number of different methods to raise offerings. As a result, the term "offering" has become widely understood as something people have to give under duress.

Knowing the Bible says that *God loves a cheerful giver*, many then started trying to be "cheerful" about taking up offerings. The problem was, they kept using the same techniques. This caused people to keep giving from the wrong motive...a guilty conscience. Historically, I believe that offering time hasn't taken on the true meaning that comes from the original context. In my studies, I discovered the Bible doesn't have a guilty connotation or tone about giving. Offerings were celebrated as a time of worship. People came before God in faith, elated about the opportunity to be part of what He was doing.

In learning to look at your offerings as investments (instead of religious sacrifices), you have to start seeing them through the spiritual law of faith. Let's go to Galatians 6:7–9, "Be not deceived; God is not mocked: for whatsoever a man soweth, that shall he also reap. For he that soweth to his flesh shall of the flesh reap corruption; but he that soweth to the Spirit shall of the Spirit reap life everlasting. And let us not be weary in well doing: for in due season we shall reap, if we faint not."

When you think of this on the positive side, it means that you don't have to reap all of the negative stuff that comes your way! You should be shouting a strong *Amen* to that! Let me tell you why I can say this...because I can just hear you saying, "Yeah, but I also have to reap the bad stuff." No, you don't...not unless you're sowing negative seeds. Galatians 3:13–14 says, "Christ hath redeemed us from the curse of the law, being made a curse for us: for it is written, Cursed is every one that hangeth on a tree..." Jesus took the penalty of the negative for you. A lot of people don't understand this. You should be able to say to the devil, "I did not sow that, so I shouldn't be receiving it as a harvest."

Deuteronomy 28:15–68 lists the negative things that don't apply to believers because Jesus was made a curse on our behalf. We have been redeemed from being cursed *going in* and *coming out,* or in any other way for that matter. Then why are so many Christians still cursed? The bottom line is, we don't know what belongs to us. Therefore, many believers don't sow in faith toward the promises of God.

- 19 -

Sowing Yields a Guaranteed Return

You must look at sowing as an investment that has to bring a return. For example, if General Motors announced, "We promise that any money you invest today will yield a fifteen percent return a year from now," everybody would knock their seats over trying to take advantage of that opportunity.

The kingdom principle is that when we sow from our substance we'll receive a one hundredfold return. (See Genesis 26:12, Matthew 19:29 and Mark 10:29–30.) We look at those Bible promises as spiritual nuances and say, "Oh, that's nice..." Other believers don't even know they are in the Bible! As a result, we don't see that giving according to biblical principles is like making a serious portfolio investment. The principle of sowing and reaping is real. Listen to me. Your scriptural investment must yield a scriptural return. If not, then your salvation is a farce.

Let me explain. As much as you know that Jesus is real and that He's your savior, you have to know that when you sow according to God's promises, you will reap. For example, people who are new in Christ might be deceived when somebody tells them, "You're not saved; you have to get baptized to get saved," or, "You have to speak in tongues to be saved." But if you've been walking with the Lord, have been studying His Word, and know the presence of God in your heart, hearing those things wouldn't be an issue for you.

You need to realize that just as Jesus promised you salvation and eternal life, He also promised an abundant return on your giving. This return is just as real as salvation, eternal life, or being filled with the Holy Spirit. Spiritual investment principles are real. They are tangible. When you sow in faith, your return is inevitable…just like going to heaven is inevitable when you die knowing Jesus as your savior.

I don't sow hoping that God might find it in His heart to bless me. I sow knowing that harvest time is surely coming—because it's based on the Word of God. He put harvesting principles into play and then said to us, "You work them." Jesus said, "…So is the kingdom of God, as if a man should cast seed into the ground; and should sleep, and rise night and day, and the seed should spring and grow up, he knoweth not how. For the earth bringeth forth fruit of herself; first the blade, then the ear, after that the full corn in the ear. But when the fruit is brought forth, immediately he putteth in the sickle, because the harvest is come" (Mark 4:26–29).

Do you understand this principle? Sowing belongs to man and the growing part is up to God. How the earth brings forth is God's part. He has promised that when you sow, He'll multiply your seeds sown. Your part is to reap the harvest. Giving unto the Lord is an investment. It must come back to you. Stop and declare this now, "It must come back to me."

A farmer won't go into the field, throw out a handful of tomato seeds in one spot, and then at harvest time say, "God didn't bless my harvest." If he did, God would ask him, "Where did you put your seeds?" "Right there." "Okay, son, where's your tomato plant?" "Right there." I can just hear God say, "Well…what did you want?" "Well, Lord, I wanted tomato plants all over the yard." To this, God would ask, "Is that where you put your seed?" You might be laughing at this story, but Christians really think this way! We want to sow sparingly and reap abundantly; sow in one place and reap all over the place. Even in natural terms, could this be possible?

We need to understand that our sowing is a spiritual investment. Let's say you bring in one hundred dollars this week. You'd pay your tithe and then sow a seed, right? After giving your tithe, what would you sow? Another ten dollars? What would you be looking for during harvest time? If that ten dollars were all you had, it would be even more significant. Remember what Jesus said about the poor widow in Mark 12? "...Verily I say unto you, That this poor widow hath cast more in, than all they which have cast into the treasury: for all *they* did cast in of their abundance; but she of her want did cast in all that she had, *even* all her living" (vv. 43–44). **Giving is about the heart, not merely the face value of the gift.**

Still, your spiritual investment must bring a return...and the amount that you reap depends on you. When I sow my seeds into the kingdom of God, I am expecting a return of one hundredfold. This isn't a whimsical thing; it's real. I've tried it. I continue to try it, and it continues to work.

- 20 -

Sowing is Strategic

Here's another angle of sowing where you want to reap. Actually, I could say it this way: Sow *what* you want to reap. Let's say you've been believing God for more favor on the job. Then you need to sow more favor towards others. Maybe you don't think your wife or husband understands you...then sow some understanding. It's that simple. **Principles of sowing bring a harvest in more than just the financial realm.** You can reap harvests in every area of your life.

Jesus said in Matthew 7:11–12, "If ye then, being evil, know how to give good gifts unto your children, how much more shall your Father which is in heaven give good things to them that ask him? Therefore all things whatsoever ye would that men should do to you, do ye even so to them: for this is the law and the prophets." He didn't say, "This is a good idea, a commandment, or something I merely suggest that you do." He was actually saying, **"This is a spiritual law."**

He also said in Luke 6:30–38, "Give to every man that asketh of thee; and of him that taketh away thy goods ask *them* not again. And as ye would that men should do to you, do ye also to them likewise....Give, and it shall be given unto you; good measure, pressed down, and shaken together, and running over, shall men give into your bosom. For with the same measure that ye mete withal it SHALL (not might) be measured to you again" (emphasis added).

God is saying that if you give to "man" (not just Christians), it will be given back to you. Some of the biggest blessings that I have received have come from people who don't know God. He'll move upon their hearts and they'll come to the church saying, "I don't know why I'm giving this to you, but here it is." It could be that afterwards they got home, thought about it, and wanted to kick themselves—but at that moment, the Spirit of God was moving upon their heart.

Other times, people will call me and say, "You helped my son, so I want to bless you. I want to give you something." Often, this comes at a strategic moment—because God knows what you need and when you're going to have need of it. When you have faithfully tithed and sown your seeds, God will cause somebody to come and pour out a blessing from heaven into your "bosom."

*Give and it shall be given...*if you want a car you should sow a car. Years ago when I needed a car, somebody gave me a car. It was run down; I didn't trust it to consistently go back and forth from Queens to Connecticut where I was working. Nevertheless, it was mine, even though I couldn't use it. My mind said, "Let somebody tow it away. I don't want it to just sit there idle." Then the Lord said to me, "No, that's your seed. Give it to somebody else."

I had options. I could have taken it to the junkyard and scrapped it for parts. I could have tried to sell it for seventy-five dollars. I could have tried to fix it up and drive it to and from work—but I didn't. God had given me clear direction. So I asked my associate if he wanted it, but he didn't need a car. I kept asking around and sure enough, I found some folks who wanted it. Then I told them, "Okay, go and get it."

Shortly afterwards, I was blessed with a new car. I could have eaten that seed, but instead, I gave it away and we ended up owning two cars. The Word of God works. His principles work...whenever we, God's covenant people, apply them.

Christians need to stop trying to make God bless us with something that we haven't sown toward receiving. If you want love, you must sow love. If you want respect, you must sow respect. If you want somebody to submit to you, you must sow submission. (A lot of people don't like that one.) If you want people to be more merciful to you, you need to sow mercy. If you want houses, sow a house. If you're sowing time, then you're going to reap time. If you knit blankets for people, one day you're going to have a lot of blankets. If you sow wealth and provision, you'll reap more of the same. **This is how sowing and reaping works.**

If you want the Father to give you good things, then give good things to others. Sow what you want to reap. Don't run to your pastor

Harvest Principle IV: Understand the Sowing Process

saying, "Wherever I go, people don't understand me; I just can't get along with them...I think they're jealous." That's not the real issue. It couldn't be true that everybody at every job you've ever had doesn't like you because they've all been jealous. Don't think you're so smart that whenever you show up at a new job, somebody isn't going to like you. Many times, when this type of situation keeps happening, you are sowing toward the problem—whether you are aware of it or not.

Everything that is in your life right now—good, bad, and indifferent—is there because of what you have sown. While this may be difficult to hear, it's the truth.

- 21 -
Sowing Multiplies and Diversifies

Let's move into another sowing principle from Ecclesiastes 11:1–4, "Cast your bread upon the waters, for you will find it after many days. Give a portion to seven, yes, even [divide it] to eight, for you know not what evil may come upon the earth. If the clouds are full of rain, they empty themselves upon the earth; and if a tree falls toward the south or toward the north, in the place where the tree falls, there it will lie. He who observes the wind [and waits for all conditions to be favorable] will not sow, and he who regards the clouds will not reap" (Ampl.).

Notice the scripture says when you cast your bread on the water you *will* (not might) find it after many days. Your "bread" isn't a loaf of stale bread that you don't want anymore. The Word isn't talking about your garbage. Your bread is your food, or your means of survival. In our case, let's say *wealth*. God is saying when we take it in our hands and throw it on the water...it will return. Pause and say this right now, "My bread will return to me after many days."

What does it mean to give a portion to seven? God is saying, "Give...give your bread in different areas, give to seven or eight." Notice that the scripture progressed from talking about casting bread on water to giving. This confirms that God isn't simply talking about throwing bread into water. He's talking about giving and sharing from what you have.

Some say, "I help my family, but I don't try to help other people. I don't know if I even want to help other people." Wait a minute. God is saying from His Word that we should spread our resources around a little bit. In other words, He's basically telling us to diversify, spread out our investments. Why? We don't know which one is going to prosper at any given time.

Many times, believers are narrow minded about the things of God. We'll say to ourselves, *I expect my blessings to come through this channel...that's how it has to come. This way and no other way.* If someone had told me that I'd go from being a computer administrator and technician making a certain amount of money to becoming a pastor of my current means, I would have said, "Oh, praise the Lord. Thank you, Jesus."—but I would no more have believed that, than if somebody would have told me I was going to fly. I had no reference for it; nevertheless, I sowed a seed. Then the Holy Spirit began to prosper me in the area of my faith, to believe beyond the level to which I had become accustomed. (He took my hand and lifted me up like the "son" in Mark 9:27.)

When I first read, "If the clouds are full of rain, they empty themselves..." I thought, *That's a silly statement...so what.* I was so wrong! I had to keep it in context. The scripture is talking about giving "to seven or eight." In this context, what is actually happening when the clouds empty themselves? The bread that you have cast on the water is coming back to you.

What does it mean for the clouds to be full? If you've sown into an area enough, no matter what that area is, when the blessing cloud becomes full...it's going to empty out. In other words, when you sow into an area enough, sooner or later you're going to get an outpouring. When the cloud gets full, it's going to empty out a one hundredfold return upon you.

Now, consider this. If you've planted a lot of seeds, you don't have time to pick yourself apart about one little thing. Pay close attention, because what's coming next is sharp, but it's good for you. When you plant a seed believing God to receive something like a car, or a house, or whatever you're believing for; if you're not careful, you'll turn that "thing" into an idol while you're believing to receive it. You'll get so caught up in the "thing" that you'll begin to put it above God. Be honest! When you hyper-focus on getting something you want, then you can start to think that God either is or isn't happy with you based on whether or not He answers this particular prayer. **Nothing in your life should have that much significance.** Nothing!

The basis for all of your giving is your covenant relationship with God. You love Him, you trust Him, you obey and get counsel from Him, and you give. You plant a seed and move on, drop another one and move on again. Then you drop yet another seed and keep moving on. You look at one area, see it growing a little bit, and then look at another that's growing a bit more...and then tend to each one. This is good, because you're focused on what God is doing in your life—not on a "thing." Stop right now and say, "Focusing on a thing is dangerous, even if God told me about it." Why? God may have told you, but He didn't ask you to help Him bring it to pass. Remember, you *sow;* God *grows.*

I'll close with Ecclesiastes 11:3–4, "If the clouds be full of rain, they empty *themselves* upon the earth: and if the tree fall toward the south, or toward the north, in the place where the tree falleth, there it shall be. He that observeth the wind shall not sow; and he that regardeth the clouds shall not reap." When you wait for things to be just right before you spread your seed around, you'll never sow...and you'll never reap. You have to sow the seed *in the season* that God is telling you to sow it. Then you can reap.

A seed planted out of season will die. You can't go out in your backyard in the middle of winter and plant corn. The natural world is a copy of the spiritual realm. That's why Jesus said, "...So is the kingdom of God, as if a man should cast seed into the ground..." (Mark 4:26). He was actually saying, "I'm telling you how the kingdom works." It's as simple as that. You must sow in obedience, in season, and in expectation toward God—and He'll give you a mighty return on your investment.

- 22 -
Sowing...the Measure of the Heart

Another important principle is found in Matthew 7:2, "...in accordance with the measure you [use to] deal out to others, it will be dealt out again to you" (Ampl.). This scripture is talking specifically about treating others right, but as I said earlier, it generally speaks to the fact that you'll get back according to what you have given. Remember the widow who gave more than everybody else when she put two mites in the offering? In giving, God is concerned with your heart, because it is in that same spirit that a harvest will be given to you.

Years ago, the best I would have been able to do for someone needing financial help would have been to give that person ten or twenty dollars...and that would have been a big thing to me—because that's all I had. As God multiplied my seeds sown, I was later able to give about four or five hundred dollars when needed, and ultimately, thousands. Is the higher amount more significant? Absolutely not. The measure of the heart is what matters most.

Let's say God used me to help meet your financial need. One day, after I helped you out according to what was in my heart, God could bless you and put you in a position to help me with multi-millions. Still, the heart is the measure. Because later, the five hundred dollars I gave to you might be worth five cents in your realm; so you'd turn around to me and say, "Pastor, I'm not going to give you just five hundred dollars...here's two million." Sowing is relative to who you are and what you have.

When your heart measure multiplies, God will get resources to you. When you get the kind of heart that wants to give God your best and help others, you're likely to become wealthy...because it blesses God when you want to be a blessing to somebody else. God will get money to you one way or the other. Yet, as long as you're thinking about you and getting only what you need—me, mine, and nobody else—God will look out for you because He loves you, but you're not going to receive real wealth.

I used to say to myself, *If I get a million dollars, it will be all mine.* It took me a while to get to the point where I was concerned for others. On one occasion God said, "If I handed you ten million dollars tomorrow, what would you do?" I said, "I'd pay my tithes, get a car, a house, some land...get both my mother and sister cars...and, oh yeah, I like this brother, so I'd give him something..." But at the same time, I was thinking, *I don't like her, so she wouldn't get anything. I'd make sure she knew I had it, but she wouldn't get anything from me.*

A few years ago when God asked me that question, I said, "Well, I'd take five million and put it into the ministry, and then I'd hire Minister So-and-so full-time so he could focus on the ministry; then I'd help Brother and Sister So-and-so get their house..." And the Lord said, "Listen to the difference in what you're saying now versus what you were saying before."

Before, I was saying what I thought God wanted to hear...then my focus was *me, me, me, my, my, my...* Now, I understand that I don't personally *need* ten million dollars, because I immediately allocated five million to others when God posed the question. God said, "Look how your heart has changed. Now, we can start talking about getting ten million to you...because your heart is different."

Most believers aren't used to having anything, so we're not trying to share too much of anything. We pat each other on the back and

Harvest Principle IV: Understand the Sowing Process

say, "I'm going to give you something…" and then we say in our own hearts…*but I'm definitely not going to help you become a millionaire.* That was my heart in the past. Now, I love to give…in a way that can change people's lives (not giving frivolously to anyone and everyone, but giving generously as the Lord leads). If I could give a million dollars to five people, I'd do it. The measure of my heart has been supernaturally expanded.

Expand your capacity to give and you'll expand your ability to receive. The measure in which you sow determines the full measure of your harvest…and as you grow in giving, it will only get better.

Harvest Time: What's That All About?

Harvest Principle IV: Understand the Sowing Process

Pray and Declare Your Harvest!

Bow your heart before the Lord and pray: "Dear Father, I lay my heart before You. Expose every hidden motive and agenda within me that would keep me from being a blessing to others. Holy Spirit, help me learn how to cast my bread upon the waters and give a portion to seven or eight. Open my eyes to see when others are in need, and open my heart to give joyfully and generously whenever and wherever You lead me.

"Help me to see that every seed I plant in Your kingdom is an investment that must bring an abundant return according to Your Word. Thank You for giving me faith that sees beyond my own needs into the supernatural realm, and that this faith causes me to invest toward fulfilling Your purpose. I know that You will multiply my seeds sown—whether they are financial, spiritual, or otherwise.

"Father God, I ask You to continue multiplying the measure of my heart in giving, and thank You for helping me to always sow in obedience, in season, and in expectation toward You. In Jesus' name. Amen."

HARVEST PRINCIPLE IV
FIVE WAYS TO UNDERSTAND THE SOWING PROCESS

Know that Your Seeds are Divine Investments
Matt. 13:44, Gal. 6:7–9

Know that Your Seeds will Yield a Guaranteed Return
Gen. 26:12, Matt. 19:29, Mk. 10:29–30, Mk. 4:26–29

Know that Your Sowing is Strategic
Matt. 7:11–12, Lk. 6:30–38

Know that You Can Multiply and Diversify Your Sowing
Eccl. 11:1–4

Know that Your Heart Determines the Measure You Sow
Matt. 7:2

Harvest Principle V

Understand the Reaping Process

- 23 -
Sow...Wait...Reap

Some people don't have a correct understanding of Matthew 6:33, "But seek ye first the kingdom of God, and his righteousness; and all these things shall be added unto you." The mistake is in thinking that they only have to be concerned about heaven; therefore, they don't have to care about feeding their families and taking care of other practical areas of life. To be honest, it took me a long time to discover the true meaning of *Seek ye first*.

I remember praying, "God, what does this verse actually mean? How am I supposed to seek Your kingdom? Where do I look in order to find it?" At that time, I thought that I had to stay in prayer twenty-four hours a day. *Surely, that's how people seek the kingdom*, I thought. Then the Lord began leading me to other scriptures like Mark 4:26, "And he said, So is the kingdom of God, as if a man should cast seed into the ground..." God also brought Matthew 13:3–4 to my attention, "...A sower went out to sow. And as he sowed, some seeds fell by the roadside..." (Ampl.).

In essence, God was saying to me, "The kingdom of God is like this: You sow, you wait, and then you reap." Remember Mark 4:28–29, "For the earth bringeth forth fruit of herself; first the blade, then the ear, after that the full corn in the ear. But when the fruit is brought forth, immediately he putteth in the sickle, because the harvest is come."

Let's follow the steps. The sower (the man) went forth to sow the seed. Once planted, the seed grew; but because the man was sleeping he didn't know how it happened (see Mark 4:27). This confirms that God is responsible for making the seeds grow. Remember, the sowing part belongs to man and the growing part belongs to God. The reaping part comes back to man, who immediately puts the sickle into the ground.

If we're honest, we'll admit that we don't always understand the reaping part. Many times, we tend to presume that God will harvest the crop for us and throw it in the barn. Sometimes we make the assumption that crops ripen and literally jump off of the branches (or out of the ground) without human intervention. This thinking is crazy! Yet, many Christians think exactly this way. Can corn jump off of the stalks, roll into the barn, and stack itself up in nice little rows? No! As "sowers," we have an obligation to go out in the field and bring in the harvest. It's our responsibility, not God's, to reap.

Harvest Principle V: Understand the Reaping Process

Don't Dig Up Your Seed

As with sowing, there are rules we must apply in order to reap successfully. If we don't reap according to the rules, we'll endanger our harvest. What do you think would happen if you planted a seed in the ground and then ripped it up as soon as a small blade broke through the soil? You'd abort the process. Then you'd have to start over again with planting. Always remember, *you sow—God grows.*

Let's say that you're believing God to give you a specific type of harvest. If you go back with your shovel and dig up that prayer request (just to see if the seed is still there or to judge for yourself how it's doing), you're in trouble. Why? You won't ruin a seed that you've planted when you pray more than once about it; but if you keep bugging God because you're not sure that He'll answer you, then do you really trust Him? (See James 1:5–7.) After a while, it will become very obvious. You didn't ask Him to help you in your unbelief so that you could continue to stand on His Word.

This takes me back to Ecclesiastes 11:3, "If the clouds be full of rain, they empty *themselves* upon the earth: and if the tree fall toward the south, or toward the north, in the place where the tree falleth, there it shall be." When you cast your bread on the water, the Word guarantees that you'll find it again *in due time.* If you've divided your seeds to *seven* or *eight*, and God is in charge of growing each seed, you won't know *which* seed in *which* place is going to be blessed first—north, south, east, or west.

Verse four goes on to say, "He that observeth the wind shall not sow; and he that regardeth the clouds shall not reap." Pay close attention to this point. There are many reasons people choose not to sow, but there are also reasons why people don't reap. Some people can deal with the wind, but not the clouds. In other words, they may have gotten past the "not sowing" obstacle, yet their harvest can still be hindered or lost if they're afraid to get out there and reap.

If you're always on the lookout for favorable conditions, you won't do what's necessary to reap a harvest. If you've grown accustomed to regarding the circumstances and conditions of your life, it will stop you from receiving God's best. One example of this is somebody who says, "Well, if my boss would just treat me right, *then I'd...*" No! Do what's right, even if the conditions don't look favorable. That's when you'll reap a rich harvest.

There will always be a reason for you to think that you shouldn't go out and get your harvest. "No way!" you might say, "Pastor, if I knew I had a harvest out there, I'd go out and get it." Oh, really? I can't tell you how many times I've had to tell people, "You need to seek the Lord and then go for it." Then they say to me, "Yes, Pastor, I know you're right...my heart bears witness, but I've been working here for fifteen years. How am I going to pay my bills?"

People don't like taking on added responsibility. They want God to take the risks, to go out in the field and bring in their harvest. Now, the day that I speak to a farmer and he or she tells me that God picked up the corn and put it in the barn, then I'll preach a different message. Until then, my position is the same. The responsibility of reaping the harvest is ours.

That's not to say that somebody won't decide to go pick some of your harvest and bring it back to you while you're working in another area. This can happen; it's an added benefit that God can grant to you for serving Him and helping other people. When you really need some help reaping, He could decide to send some help your way. Remember Luke 6:38? If you give to others as unto the Lord, God will use those same people to pour a part of your harvest right into your bosom...and this usually happens when you need it most.

- 24 -

Reap in the Spirit

The spiritual realm is more powerful than the natural realm. So it doesn't make sense for God to lead you into blessing if you still have a poverty mentality—because as soon as you reap your harvest, you'll turn it into lack. Read the story of the prodigal son in Luke 15:12–17. Your heart must be changed first. If your perception of yourself is still at minimum wage, welfare checks, and receiving food stamps, it doesn't make sense for God to give you five million dollars. It wouldn't be long before the entire amount was gone and you were right back on food stamps.

I've watched many biography specials about recording stars that once had big hit records, fame, and fortune, only to discover that some of them ended up as clerks at their local convenience store or doing door-to-door product sales. In short, they landed right back where they started. Very few that attained success enjoyed the fruits of ongoing success. Most squandered their riches and ended up broke again.

In order to reap effectively, there must first be a change in your perception of who you are in the Spirit. You have to know what is truly yours and understand the greatness of God's calling on your life. Otherwise, there's no sense in taking you into a Promised Land that you're not going to be able to maintain.

I came to understand something from reading 1 Corinthians 10:13, "...God *is* faithful, who will not suffer you to be tempted above that ye are able..." By and large, people tend to equate this verse with pain and suffering. Not me. When I applied it to sowing and reaping, it literally came to life because it told me that God wouldn't ever put me in a situation that was going to overwhelm me.

In other words, God isn't likely going to "bless" somebody who once had a recurring liquor habit with a job in a liquor factory. We put too much on ourselves. I've heard people say things like, "Well, I think God put me here so that I could be a testimony to others about how God brought me out." Many times, these same people end up becoming testimonies to the Alcoholics Anonymous motto, "Once an alcoholic always an alcoholic." Don't get me wrong; I'm not saying God would never send someone that has come through a situation back into a similar situation, in order to win others for Christ. My point is, we too easily get ourselves into difficulties and then try to turn them around to become what we want them to be, not what they're supposed to be according to the will of God.

Our hearts can deceive us; especially where financial sowing and reaping are concerned. This makes it extremely important for us to seek God concerning the state of our hearts and where we should be reaping. Then we can reap the full increase of what He gives.

- 25 -

Reap in Season

One day while sorting through some old things, I discovered that years before I had been standing in faith to purchase a house without a loan. In retrospect, I immediately realized that I hadn't really been standing. I was merely confessing. Read these words carefully: *Your harvest isn't automatic. You have to go out and bring it in.*

Let's look at a biblical example. When God brought the children of Israel out of Egypt into the wilderness, they started crying for food as soon as they ran out of reserves. So God rained down manna from heaven and it fell all over the ground. Can you imagine food actually dropping down on you from heaven? Yet even in performing this amazing miracle, God still instructed the people to gather it! Today's

Harvest Time: What's That All About?

Christian would say, "No! We're just supposed to sit back and declare, 'I believe it's mine; come to me now, manna, in the name of Jesus.'"

This isn't how things worked in the Bible. The Israelites had to go out with their baskets, get on the ground and gather up enough manna for an entire day. Manna didn't fall straight into their mouths and instantly fill them up. (See Exodus 16:13–17.)

A harvest has to be reaped! This doesn't mean you should run around like crazy "in your flesh" trying to reap a harvest in your own power. There is a balance. In the Spirit realm (as well as in the natural), you have to get in the right posture through prayer so that you'll know where you need to be and when God needs you to be there. Then you can go and pick up the provision...just like you would go to the grocery store and carry bags of groceries back to your home.

Let me use another analogy from the Lord, because I'm sure that we've all experienced this. Let's say that you went to the supermarket expecting to buy a couple of things and ended up buying much more. You'd come out, loaded down with bags, realizing that you don't have a shopping cart. Struggling not to drop anything, you'd try to get the groceries to the car without ruining them...so you'd walk a few steps and then sit down, and then you'd walk another few steps, sit down again, and so on. One way or another, you'd be determined to get your groceries home.

Spiritual reaping is very much like that. Sometimes, you have to pick up your harvest and start making your way home while demons are jumping in front of you, waving and throwing up their hands, throwing snowballs and all kinds of other junk your direction. Every now and then you have to stop, catch your breath, regain your balance, and keep moving toward your goal. Remember, you don't have to fight against the devil—he's already defeated. He's just trying to psyche you out. Knowing this, don't move away from your blessings. Don't leave them behind. Keep them close while you rest, and then pick up your bags again until you get them all the way to the car, and ultimately...to your home.

You have to learn how to reach into the spirit realm and reap. Close your eyes a moment and just reach in...grab your expected harvest and pull it toward you. Don't just sit around and make confessions. To reap effectively, you have to stay in a posture to hear from God, see the harvest in your spirit, and then actually go out by faith to receive it and bring it home. I can think of many times when I just sat in my living room crying and praying...and when I finally got the revelation from God, He was saying, "Get up and go out." This happened when the Israelites were crying out to be delivered from Egypt, "Oh, God, we don't want to be in slavery anymore. We need You..." Then God sent Moses saying, "Get up and get out of Egypt."

You are believing God for deliverance, so He's not going to treat you like a slave—even while you're still living in lack. Get out of that place! Get up and leave. When God releases direction in your spirit, it's time to go. For many of us, that is the moment when fear sets in, "Well, I don't want to leave; the Egyptians feed me well. How am I going to eat if I go out there?" That's what the Israelites did. They got half way out into the wilderness, started running low on provisions, and immediately started complaining, "It was better when we were in Egypt. Maybe we should go back."

They were so accustomed to being slaves that they didn't want to take responsibility and take advantage of the new freedom that God had given them. Therefore, they couldn't see the harvest.

Most of the original generation died in the wilderness—they missed going into the Promised Land because of their own lack of faith, desire, and action. God was showing them how to get their harvest and had given them the perfect opportunity. But they didn't want to rise up out of a poverty mentality and reap what was already theirs. Therefore, they couldn't see that God had already equipped them to do something they'd never done before…*get up and take a new land*.

It was never God's intention to simply drop the Promised Land down from heaven. He gave the Israelites manna, quail, a glory cloud, and pillars of fire to help them follow Him closely every day in order to reach their destination. What more did they need? There's a process in going from where you are to your land of promise, and if you'll stay in the posture to receive from God and act on His direction alone—you'll reap. Say this out loud, "There's a process for me to go from where I am into what God has promised me. I'm going to go all the way through and reap my harvest."

- 26 -
Refuse to Receive Anything from the Devil

It's easy to believe that reaping our harvest is somehow dependent on God, upon what His mood might be at any given moment. That's a lie from the enemy. The size of your harvest depends on your heart and the "measure" with which you sow. If you believe anything else, you're playing directly into the devil's hand. Focus on the positives, and know that you're going to reap what you sow! This positive reality is powerful. Don't just sit around doing nothing because you're worried about sowing something negative and reaping a curse instead of a blessing. Sow your heart into God and then do what He tells you to do. It's that simple.

Christians shouldn't preach the devil's gospel. God said that you're going to reap only what you sow. Apply this spiritual knowledge correctly. If you focus on sowing good things unto the Lord, that's all you're going to reap! Nothing and nobody can change this reality: not a demon, not your grandfather, grandmother, uncle, or anyone else. I don't care if a curse has been running in your family for seventy-five years. The Word is far more powerful.

When you know that you are in a right relationship with God and the devil tries to come and mess with you, don't immediately think you have to start "binding" him. Instead, just give him that look...you know what I mean; like that look you flash when your child is doing something that he or she needs to stop...*right now.* (Smile.) When you shoot that look, your child immediately knows, *I'd better stop.* Seriously, though, you can get to a place in your walk with God that when the enemy shows up you simply resist him (i.e., give him that look)...and he'll back up.

God said not to be deceived...you're going to reap from the faithful actions that you sow! Therefore, you should expect to receive the best. If the UPS man came to your door today with a box of manure, you wouldn't sign for it, would you? On the spiritual level, some people might take that package in their houses and say, "Lord, are you trying to show me something?" Not me. I won't sign for it. I don't want it. And if that UPS man comes back five more times with that same package, my answer to him will be the same, "No, I don't receive it, I won't have it, and if you come to my door again I might decide to hurt you..." You don't have to sign for the toxic junk that the enemy keeps trying to leave at your door.

Bear with me for pushing the envelope a little bit to help you understand where you are and what you're willing to accept. You don't have to say yes to everything! I don't know about you, but I'm not trying to learn by getting my head bonked. My prayer is, "Instruct me, Lord, that I might do right." I'm not trying to learn through pain, suffering, and hard times. Those days are over for me. When the enemy comes, I say, "Lord, is there something I'm doing that's wrong?" If He doesn't tell me where I need to be corrected, then I don't accept the package—because I believe my Father is the ultimate teacher.

The Bible challenges us that if our children ask for fish, would we give them serpents? (See Luke 11:11.) Of course, not! God doesn't send hard times because He's trying to teach us something. We have hard experiences because we give them place through our own disobedience. God is simply trying to teach us that we are being destroyed for lack of knowledge (Hosea 4:6). The devil simply doesn't have the right to inflict whatever he desires upon you.

Listen to me. You're supposed to be able to pay your bills, eat, and at least have some surplus…at a minimum! I'm not saying that you have to own a Mercedes or possess other luxury items—but if you're constantly struggling to pay your bills, something's wrong. God has promised to be your provider. He has promised to feed and take care of you, even if you're in a bad state. For example, when my son has bad grades, he's still going to dress better than most of the kids on the block, *because that's my boy*. When my son goes out, he represents me.

The devil has lied to God's people so successfully that many have concluded God is constantly looking for opportunities to take blessings away from us. No! He wants to bless us! If you make a mistake and then repent, God will restore you. That means He'll set you up to continue prospering and moving forward.

Remember James 1:5, "If any of you lack wisdom, let him ask of God, that giveth to all *men* liberally, and upbraideth not…" The word *upbraid* means "to find fault" (Strong's 3679, Gk.). If you lack wisdom…if you've made a mistake or gotten out of the will of God, ask God and He will generously give you the wisdom that you need to get a breakthrough without harping on your faults. God will never say, "Well, I would help you, but because you did thus and so, I'm upset with you." When you repent and ask for wisdom, God will never find fault with you. He'll give you wisdom, liberally—that means "spread all out" (Strong's 574, Gk.).

So, if I get an unexpected package, I seek God and then do one of two things. If He shows me that I'm wrong about something, I do some plowing and repent. If not, I rest in the fact that I'm submitted to God; then I resist the devil and keep moving toward my harvest.

Harvest Time: What's That All About?

Harvest Principle V: Understand the Reaping Process

Pray and Declare Your Harvest!

Say this right now, "The devil is a liar and I'm coming for my stuff." If he's been trying to push you around, it's time to take back your harvest. Reach up and take the hem of Jesus' garment…

Declare in the Spirit, "I accept the blessings of God. I accept correction from God. I am a sheep, I know His voice intimately, and the voice of a stranger I will not follow. The accuser will not lead me. I will not be moved by guilt and shame. I will be moved by the liberal, non-upbraiding voice of my loving Father, Almighty God. In Jesus' name, Amen." **So Be It!**

HARVEST PRINCIPLE V
FOUR WAYS TO UNDERSTAND THE REAPING PROCESS

Understand that You Sow, God Grows, and You Reap
Mk. 4:28–29, Matt. 13:3–4, Eccl. 11:3

Understand Who You Are in the Spirit
Lk. 15:12–17

Understand How to Reap in Season
Ex. 16:13–17

Refuse to Receive Anything from the Devil
Lk. 11:11, Hos. 4:6, Jms. 1:5–7

Harvest Principle VI

Guard Against Losses

- 27 -
No Seed, No Godly Harvest

God is consistent. He'll keep coming to you with the same thing from every side: front, back, right and left, until you finally get it. With this in mind, let's examine the common mistakes that can hinder your harvest by looking at the two most common problem areas: *no harvest* and *small harvest*. Remember, I'm not talking about tithing. Tithing is not sowing. You "sow" offerings after you've set the right environment by giving your tithes.

The number one reason that people receive *no harvest* from God is they have planted *no seed*. This sounds pretty straightforward, but let me clarify. When you don't sow a seed, you won't get the harvest that you desire. Instead, you'll reap a poverty harvest…the result of unbelief. The other type, *small harvest*, means that you're receiving a harvest, but it's not according to the one hundredfold return that the Bible promises.

Some people say that lack of faith can cause you not to reap a godly harvest. This is true only on the back end, because if you've planted a seed and then dig it back up, it demonstrates that you don't trust God to grow it. Right now, I'm focusing on the front end. If you have faith in God, but still don't plant any seed in the ground, all of the faith in the world isn't going to bring you a godly harvest. Let me put it this way; if you don't plant tomato seeds in the ground, you're not going to reap tomatoes. You'll get grass, weeds, or whatever would naturally grow in that place without your contribution.

A lot of Christians think they can simply believe that they've received a harvest, and then confess they've received it, and the harvest will come. This was prevalent when the "word of faith" message became popular. People were declaring, "If I speak to this mountain and say, 'Be thou removed,' I'll have whatever I say. So I declare right now…that's *my wife*, *my car*, *my job*…" I'm not exaggerating—because I was one of them.

Before this, I had been taught, "When God wants you to have it, He'll give it to you." So I had started out in my Christian walk believing the opposite: I personally didn't have anything to do with bringing in my harvest. Therefore, I believed that whatever came to me was based solely on the kindness of God's heart. So when I received something from Him, I rationalized that I'd either prayed loudly enough or cried long enough to release His compassion.

I was under the false impression that I had to become desperate and pitiful before God would help me. I actually believed that if I kept running away from God, like the prodigal son ran away from his father, one day (like what happened in that story) He'd end up receiving me back home, putting a gold ring on my finger, and so on (Luke 15:11–22). I actually thought, *Maybe if I get so messed up and end up in a pigsty, God will help me out.* I didn't see the fact that the son rose up out of his mess and ran back home to his father.

In the end, it didn't matter whether I was confessing, groveling, or rolling around in the dirt. The result was the same. I didn't get the harvest that I was hoping to receive. Nobody told me during these seasons of lack that I needed to actually sow some seed.

Some believers constantly pray for God to bless them, but they won't release what they have in their hands. That's *regarding the clouds*...making every excuse why they can't plant a seed *now*. Let's see if scripture bears this out by going back to the sixth chapter of Luke. (And by the way, this verse appears in red, which means that Jesus said it.) Verse 38 starts off by saying, "Give, and it shall be given unto you..." Let's contrast this by stating the opposite. "Don't give and it [a good measure] shall not be given unto you..." Could this be any simpler?

- 28 -

Guard Against an Impatient Heart

If you're impatient, you can forfeit your harvest. Galatians 6:7–9 says, "Be not deceived; God is not mocked: for whatsoever a man soweth, that shall he also reap. For he that soweth to his flesh shall of the flesh reap corruption; but he that soweth to the Spirit shall of the Spirit reap everlasting life. And let us not be weary in well doing: for in due season we shall reap, if we faint not."

A lot of people quit just before their harvest comes. They initially believed the Word of God and faithfully tithed and sowed. Then they waited and waited, and it seemed like nothing was ever going to happen. That's usually when people come to me and say, "Well, Pastor, I claimed it fifteen times and I still didn't see the manifestation...so I quit." They planted, watered, and then afterwards got tired of waiting for God to complete the growth process. Weary of standing and believing God, they stopped short of doing what's right in His eyes until their harvest came. They didn't stay before Him in prayer in order to reap their harvest (remember, we must reap in the Spirit first). If God were to send a courier to their doorsteps with a package from heaven, they would have already moved without leaving a forwarding address.

Let's read verse seven from the Amplified version, "Do not be deceived {and} deluded {and} misled; God will not allow Himself to be sneered at (scorned, disdained, or mocked by mere pretensions or professions, or by His precepts being set aside.) [He inevitably deludes himself who attempts to delude God.] For whatever a man sows, that {and} that only is what he will reap." The devil will try to deceive you by confusing the true meaning of this verse. Yet, understand that God isn't going to let the devil, you, or anybody else make a fool out of Him by saying that His precepts don't work. Never give up before the manifestation! Don't say, "Well, Pastor, I waited and waited, and prayed and prayed...I guess it just isn't God's will for me." When you do this, you're letting go of the promises of God!

Stop and say this out loud, "My harvest is spiritual." We do not start by reaping in the natural realm because we're sowing in obedience to supernatural principles. When you give, it's a supernatural act. On the other hand, when you deposit your money in the bank, that's a natural act. It's common to man. And the return you will receive from that deposit is also common—you'll wait thirty days or more to gain an average of two percent interest, and think that you're really gaining something.

God's kingdom promises a one hundredfold return on your seeds sown (remember Genesis 26:12). This is a lot better than the return on any bank account or worldly investment that I've ever seen. Natural principles are merely a shadow of spiritual realities. Let's say that you still feel more secure putting all of your money in a bank because it promises to yield a certain return over time. There's a chance you might get that return, and there's also a chance you might not. What if your bank goes out of business? Sure, you can get the insured portion of your funds back from the government in due time, but immediately afterwards you'll have to find another bank to give you another two percent.

Spiritual truths are definite. They are more real than what you can see, hear, smell, taste, and touch. Spiritual truths never change. Stand on His promises and endure the "light afflictions" of this life according to 2 Corinthians 4:18, "Since we consider {and} look not to the things that are seen but to the things that are unseen; for the

Harvest Principle VI: Guard Against Losses

things that are visible are temporal (brief and fleeting), but the things that are invisible are deathless {and} everlasting" (Ampl.).

Everything that you can see, hear, touch, and smell was first spiritual before it manifested in the natural realm. Therefore, before you go to purchase a car, you have to have a vision of what you want and the kind of deal you're looking for. It's the same with sowing and reaping in the Spirit. You must have a vision in the spirit realm before going forward in the natural to start putting that thing together.

Here's a news flash: Man didn't create anything. We discover things. When you hear that someone invented something, it really means that he or she is the first one to discover it. For example, scientists discovered an ore called *metal* when melting down a mountain's core. Anything you can think of—metal, food, plastics, Pentium computers—all of these resources have been available in a simple, "undiscovered" form since the beginning of time. This means Adam and Eve could have had the most advanced Pentium computers in the Garden of Eden if they had wanted to—though in their perfected state, they most likely didn't need computers. All of God's vast resources are already in the earth in an unseen state...man didn't create anything.

Why, then, do we try to create our own harvests? Why do we give up before God (Who created everything we know or could ever imagine) brings the manifestation?

As I said before, the fact that we're going to reap what we sow is a godly promise. Don't be deceived. Don't let the devil fool you, and don't listen to lies and false reports you may hear from other people. You will get what you sow—a harvest of good things will come if you sow according to godly principles. Your expected return is on the way, so don't lose hope. Don't become faint and let go of God's promises. Be patient while God grows your seeds. Keep holding on. Don't give up.

Obviously, things will come to try your faith. That's why the scriptures constantly encourage God's people to have faith in God and never give up. What would happen if a farmer planted seeds and waited patiently as the seasons passed...and then over time he became discouraged because he didn't see things happening the way he originally expected? If he got tired of waiting, and then packed up and moved away from the farm, he'd be leaving behind a harvest. When the crops ultimately sprouted up, he wouldn't be there to reap or enjoy them. Have you ever done this?

Harvest Time: What's That All About?

This is why Galatians 6:9 teaches, "And let us not be weary in well doing: for in due season we shall reap, if we faint not." It says we SHALL reap; not *might*. There's not just a fifty-fifty chance that you're going to get a return—YOU WILL GET A HARVEST on the godly seeds that you sow. The condition is, DON'T FAINT. Your due season is coming.

I've heard two different well-known preachers give their definitions of "due season." One said, "When it happens..." Another said, "A little bit longer than you want it to be." Why would "due season" be a little bit longer than what you'd want? *Your flesh wants the harvest, now*. That's why I say "due season" is just long enough to get the flesh out the way so that the Spirit of God can move. If you don't lose heart, you WILL reap.

Know the State of Your Flocks

Another way to exercise patience in reaping your harvest is to know the state of your flocks. This not only deals with *where* you've sown, but *what* you've sown. You shouldn't just throw your cash into a bucket and watch it go down the aisle without accounting for it. Years ago, I started reviewing every tithe that I'd ever paid and any seed that I'd sown...to anybody, anywhere...anything that came to mind, including material things: computers, cars, toys, coats, belts, a tie...anything.

I'm not trying to be legalistic in mentioning this process, nor am I on a witch-hunt. And just to be clear, I'm definitely not trying to make you feel condemned if you haven't worked through this process. However, you should have at least a general idea of *what* you give and *where* you're giving it. How are you going to know what's supposed to be in your orchard if you don't remember *what* you planted *where*?

You could be praying for a harvest that's already manifested—but because you forgot *what* you sowed *where*, you can't reap it. This means there could be big, fat, juicy harvests just sitting out there waiting for you. Remember, spiritual things don't die. You've tithed, so your fruits have been protected, which means they won't rot in the field. God has already rebuked the devourer, so the harvest is just sitting there...waiting for you. If your crops could talk, they'd be saying, "Would you please come and get the fruit off of me? I want to bear some more fruit." If this doesn't get you excited, you need to be born again!

Take a moment and consider this, because when you know (or at least have a good idea) what type of harvest that you're believing for, you can stand firm and not faint. When you know what's due to you from the seeds that you've sown, you can be vigilant and diligent in faith to stand for what already belongs to you. If you've sown seeds and faithfully done everything you know to do, your harvest is sitting on the vines just waiting for you to come and start reaping in tractor-trailer truckloads. Never give up and walk away with your harvest still in the field.

This should make you want to get on your face before God and say, "Okay, Lord, show me where my harvest is."

Romans 11:29 says, "...the gifts and calling of God *are* without repentance." Specifically, it speaks about the restoration of Israel, but the general principle is this: God doesn't decree a gift to you and then turn around and say He made a mistake and take it back. Are you filled with the Holy Ghost? If so, have you sinned since being filled? Did God take that gift back? No! It's yours. God is not a man and He will not lie. He promised that if you sow, that and *that only* shall you reap.

If you know the state of your flocks and you're expecting a biblical return, you can be certain when some of your harvest is missing. Take a spiritual inventory. Be certain of what's due to you.

When you are in error, the enemy can come and take what God has given you. The Bible says not to let anybody fool you; God won't be sneered at, because His law of sowing and reaping is real. (See Galatians 6:7.) You can be saved and fail to sow good things, and you will reap the results. This is also why unsaved people can do wicked things and still prosper. In fact, even though they don't know God some are big givers. When you start looking at how much some of the wealthiest, most prominent recording artists give to help others, it clears up this issue. Yet eventually, if they remain in sin they'll die without Christ, because evil has to reap evil. No Christian should want someone to die in his or her sin, nor should we be satisfied to leave this earth without reaping the full harvest that God has given us.

So there are people working the principle of sowing and reaping while yet doing evil, and the principle still works. Matthew 5:45 says, "...for he maketh his sun to rise on the evil and on the good, and sendeth rain on the just and on the unjust." This means that I could go into my backyard and plant vegetables and an unsaved person could do the same in his or her yard—and both gardens would flourish if we followed the laws. God's laws are real! He doesn't suspend them simply because He may not be pleased with something you've done, or if another person doesn't know Him. In fact, this is also why our heavenly Father can also choose to bless you even in your mess.

Why should you live a righteous life? Why should you consistently plow up the impurities in the soil of your heart? As a child of God, your love for Him should make you want to please Him in every way—and the Holy Spirit will empower you to do what is pleasing to God as you walk in obedience. If you keep living in sin, however, the devil will try to steal everything that God has given you because he hates the Father and wants to discredit His Word. Satan, the accuser of the brethren, will try to convince you that God has forsaken you so that you'll give up, walk away from God, and miss reaping your harvest. Be patient, trust God, and you will reap.

- 29 -

Guard Against Laziness

You can lose your godly harvest if you're too lazy to reap. This is why you have to be able to discern the difference between a blessing and a miracle.

Let me explain. Many times, you can get yourself in a messy situation and God will bless you anyway. For example, let's say that somebody supernaturally helped you out of a financial bind. You'd probably say, "I didn't know how I was going to pay my bills, Pastor, and then somebody knocked on the door with a bag of groceries." Glory to God! God moved for you in His miracle power. And, yes, it blessed you tremendously. Yet to be accurate, I would have to call this a supernatural intervention.

Believers aren't supposed to live from miracle to miracle. We shouldn't be getting ourselves into such a bind that God has to suspend the laws of nature just to send a bird to bring us a bag of food. Now, if you're in a situation that you have no choice in the matter, like being stuck in a remote location in Africa or being locked up in a Communist country, God may have to perform supernatural miracles to bring you out. In our day-to-day lives, however, we shouldn't sit idly by (spiritually or otherwise) expecting answers to come knocking at our door.

We need to get to the place that we are constantly giving, sowing, knowing the state of our flocks, and going forward doing things in partnership with God. Be "instant" in and out of season (see 2 Timothy

4:2). If He says, "When you get to this corner, turn left and go up the stairs...that's where your blessing is going to be," you should be obedient to His voice. It's that simple. When God speaks, it doesn't always have to be a super-spiritual, falling down through the ceiling type of experience. "Pastor, I was sitting in my room; the lightening flashed, the ceiling opened up, and my rent money was just laying on the table!" We need to get to the point where we're progressively involved in manifesting the blessings of God—not just in our own lives, but also in the lives of those around us.

Some people think that harvest is automatic. They think that if you sow your seed, pray and confess, that God will bless you. Consider again how the Israelites received manna from heaven. Every morning, they still had to reap it. The fact that God supernaturally provided food from heaven was definitely a miracle...but that wasn't the end of it. God told Moses that the people had to gather the manna, bring it home, prepare it, and then eat it. God didn't just drop the manna into their stomachs and fill them supernaturally. They had to gather the manna and bring it home. If the Israelites hadn't acted according to their faith, they would have been crying with no food.

Proverbs 10:4 says, "He becomes poor who works with a slack *and* idle hand, but the hand of the diligent makes rich" (Ampl.). Thank God for miracles...but make a decision to be a person of blessing. Go out and reap that harvest!

- 30 -

Small Seed, Small Harvest

If you don't sow, you won't reap what you desire. If you sow a little, you'll get a little. We read about this in 2 Corinthians 9:6–7, "[Remember] this: he who sows sparingly *and* grudgingly will also reap sparingly *and* grudgingly, and he who sows generously [that blessings may come to someone] will also reap generously *and* with blessings. Let everyone [give] as he has made up his own mind *and* purposed in his own heart, not reluctantly *or* sorrowfully or under compulsion, for God loves (He takes pleasure in, prizes above all other things, and is unwilling to abandon or to do without) a cheerful (joyous, prompt to do it) giver [whose heart is in his giving]" (Ampl.). I don't need to elaborate.

You might say, "I understand, Pastor, but I don't have that much to give. After I pay my bills, I don't have any money. It's kind of hard for me to give." Let's continue with verse 8, "And God is able to make all grace (every favor and earthly blessing) come to you in abundance, so that you always *and* under all circumstances *and* whatever the need be self-sufficient (see that) [possessing enough to require no aid or support and furnished in abundance for every good work and charitable donation]."

I believe some Christians read this verse and think that God is supposed to bring blessings to them. The context of this verse focuses on what happens when *a believer* gives. It's not talking about getting without first giving. Do you also notice from verse 8 that God's blessings always seem to be mixed with your ability to bless someone else?

Let's keep reading, "As it is written, He [the benevolent person] scatters abroad; he gives to the poor; His deeds of justice *and* goodness *and* kindness *and* benevolence will go on *and* endure forever. And [God] Who provides seed for the sower and bread for eating will also provide and multiply your [resources for] sowing and increase the fruits of your righteousness [which manifests itself in active goodness, kindness, and charity]" (vv. 9–10, Ampl.).

Don't Eat Your Seed

God is saying, "If you don't have seed, I'll give you seed." This is another area where a lot of people get messed up—because they haven't yet learned how to discern their need from their seed.

Let me give you an example. There was a time when I didn't have any money, so I got on my face and prayed. I was believing God for my first job, and I needed to earn around thirty thousand dollars a year. After I sought the Lord, He blessed me with a one-day job. For that one day of work I made seventy-five dollars. Was my prayer answered for the thirty thousand dollar job? No. God blessed me with seventy-five dollars for one day's work.

I could have said, "Good, now we can get some groceries..." Actually, I wasn't sure exactly what I was going to do with what I had earned, but since I didn't have any money, seventy-five dollars was a lot. In fact, I had to break one of the twenty-dollar bills to go home on the train.

Was my need being met, or was that seventy-five dollars a seed for me to sow? I had to make that decision. Most people would have thought; *I have seventy-five dollars. I guess God is just giving me this money so that I'll have something to spend until I get a permanent job.* Not me. I prayed and God said, "Don't eat all of that." So I bought a Metro Card to have transportation for the week, which was about fifteen dollars, and then I got a few groceries. I had twenty-five dollars left.

Then I remembered a woman named Sister Wyrema from Africa, so I went to my pastor and asked, "When is Sister Wyrema coming back to the church?" He said, "She's not going to stop here." I said, "Well, when you see her, please give her this offering and tell her to pray with me for the job that I've been believing God for." He put the offering in his pocket and forgot all about it until he was driving Sister Wyrema to the airport. This will show you how strongly God feels about your seed. As they were driving, out of the blue she said, "How's that brother doing?" He replied, "Which brother?" "The guy with the long braid. He's on my heart…how is he?" Then he remembered, "Oh, I've got twenty-five dollars in my pocket that I'm supposed to give to you from him."

Later, she told me that she took the twenty-five dollars, put it in her Bible, and said to God, "I will not spend this money until I hear that his prayer has been answered." A couple of weeks later, I was working at the job I wanted for the salary that I had been believing for! God gave me a harvest proportionate to my seed for that season of my life.

- 31 -

Guard Against Selfishness

When you sow only for what God can do for you (not out of love, obedience, and expectation toward Him), your harvest will be small. Proverbs 11:24 says, "There are those who [generously] scatter abroad, and yet increase more; there are those who withhold more than is fitting or what is justly due, but it results only in want" (Ampl.).

Let's look again at 2 Corinthians 9:6–7, "…he who sows sparingly *and* grudgingly will also reap sparingly *and* grudgingly, and he who sows generously [that blessings may come to someone] will also reap generously *and* with blessings. Let each one [give] as he has made up his own mind…" (Ampl.). I've already mentioned how some people think this verse means they don't have to tithe ten percent of their income to God. He also showed me another principle from this scripture: You're not supposed to sow just to be blessed. You sow for someone else to be blessed. That's the balance.

Harvest Time: What's That All About?

According to spiritual law, you'll be blessed when you give—but don't let that be your motivation. Never give under compulsion (an outside impulse that literally forces you to do something that's not in your spirit). Let me explain. I've been in services where pastors have stood up and said, "Now, we're going to raise money for this building…if you really love the Lord and want to see this happen, then we need you to give from your heart." What's really happening is they're extorting you from the pulpit. They're making you feel guilty so that if you don't give, you'll feel like you don't really love God. Let me say this: If you give in that kind of offering, you might as well throw it in the garbage, because that's not joyful giving—that's compulsion! Selfishness can happen on both sides of the pulpit.

On another occasion while I was visiting a church, I was compelled in my spirit to write a two thousand dollar check during the offering. Then the pastor got up and started asking for two hundred dollar seeds, saying, "I just need fifty people…" and so on. He kept pushing the people, "Now, I'm not going to move until I see fifty people give a two hundred dollar seed." My spirit was grieved, so I tore up that check and wrote a two hundred dollar offering. *I was going to give two thousand and he talked it down to two hundred trying to get people to give in a grudging way.* The offering I gave was a mercy gift. While I was giving it, I prayed, "God, when he touches this check let his heart be convicted, because his spirit is wrong."

On the other hand, some people feel like they have to let everybody know what they're doing. If somebody in our church tried to get the microphone and say, "Pastor, I just want to say that I've got a seed for you today." My response would be, "Go sit down somewhere and take your seed with you. I'm not impressed with that." It's selfish…bottom line.

I believe if people are taught about harvesting, nothing can stop them from giving. I even encourage the members of our church to give to each other. They don't always have to give their offerings directly to the church! Sometimes people need to give their seed to somebody else, so that the left hand doesn't know what the right hand is doing (Matthew 6:1–4). It's good to find a brother or sister and let the Lord use you to bless them from your heart.

The problem comes when we look for reasons not to sow. We think, *Should I give or shouldn't I give? What should or shouldn't I do? Well, I know God is leading me to give something to this person. Should I give ten or twenty dollars? I really need the other ten. Maybe*

Harvest Principle VI: Guard Against Losses

I should give ten...but if I pray long enough...okay, God just gave me peace to give five.

One morning, I got excited about sowing as I was praying on my way to church. It just came up in me. I said to God, "I want to give my car to...because they're moving to Connecticut and will need it." God directed me to stop and pray more about it. "Let Me do what I'm trying to do," He said. "You're trying to jump in, and sometimes you get in the way of what I'm doing. I know your heart means well, but just slow down a minute and pray." So that's what I did.

Do you see the difference? You'll either be in the place where you're trying to find a reason to sow, or God has brought you to the place where He has to give you reasons not to sow. When you get to the place where you always want to give to others, God will have to say, "Just slow down...stop." That's prosperity in the truest sense. Why? You're not prosperous if you don't have a giver's heart. You may have acquired a few things, but remember, the Bible says it's better to give than to receive (Acts 20:35).

The more you pray for a heart to give, the more prosperous you'll become, because the Word has promised to bring an abundant return upon a giving heart. So instead of praying for *getting*, we need to be praying for the gift (or the anointing) of *giving*. (See Romans 12:8.) Prosperity isn't about believing for what we want to be ours...it's about saying, "Lord, I want to bless somebody else."

Remember 2 Corinthians 9:7, "Let each one [give] as he has made up his own mind *and* purposed in his heart, not reluctantly *or* sorrowfully or under compulsion, for God loves (He takes pleasure in, prizes above other things, and is unwilling to abandon or do without) a cheerful (joyous 'prompt to do it') giver [whose heart is in his giving]" (Ampl.). When you give because you feel like you have to, you're not going to reap abundantly with blessings. Don't get me wrong...if you sow, you're going to reap, but again—your heart determines the measure.

You could give twenty dollars with a pure heart saying, "This is all I've got, God, but I'm giving my all to You," and He could multiply that twenty dollars a thousandfold! It doesn't say anywhere in the Bible that we're "limited to" one hundredfold returns. In fact, I heard once that a hundredfold return doesn't necessarily mean one hundred times the amount of your offering. It means *the best possible yield.* In other words, one hundred percent is the best possible outcome. Understood within this context, a one hundredfold return on twenty dollars could be two million.

God's focus is not about money, He's focused on a joyous *prompt to do it* giver whose heart is at the center of his giving. Don't be selfish. God blesses you so that you'll keep on giving. He'll make every heavenly blessing come to you so that you can be a storehouse of blessing for somebody else—and in the process, you will be richly blessed.

- 32 -
Guard Against Carelessness

When you fail to discern your seed, you'll limit the size of your harvest. Let's keep moving through 2 Corinthians 9 to verse 8, "And God is able to make all grace (every favor and earthly blessing) come to you in abundance, so that you may be always *and* under all circumstances *and* whatever the need be self-sufficient [possessing enough to require no aid or support and furnished in abundance for every good work and charitable donation]" (Ampl.).

This reminds me of something that relates to this verse in the natural realm. I've had people come to me and say, "Pastor, I don't like Republicans because they're messing with the money for college." Here's my response. The Bible seems to say that if you're right with God, you won't need grants. I don't label myself as a Republican or a Democrat...I'm a Christian. But let me say this: When you get caught up in the system's ability to meet your needs, you just revealed who your God is.

Second Corinthians 9:8 says that God is able to make every favor and earthly blessing come to you in abundance so that you will always, in every circumstance—whatever the need may be—have enough so that you don't require aid or support. God blesses you so that you can be a blessing.

Many believers say; "God is able, Pastor." What they really mean when they say this is usually quite the opposite. Often, they've distorted and twisted God's Word and made it into a lie. What they really mean to say is, though God is able, He's just not willing *right now*. "Oh, Pastor, in His timing...because He's able." When you say this, you're actually saying that you're ready and that you've got your act together; God just needs to get His act together and catch up with you, in order to get you that blessing. Do you see how careless this is in expressing your faith toward God?

You may not want to say *Amen* to that, but it's the truth. The church has to get rid of all the phony stuff. Knowing that God is able isn't a step of faith. Knowing that He's willing *and* able to do it for you...that's a step of faith. Simply saying that God is able doesn't mean you agree with the fact that He wants you to reap a harvest. Here's an example. At this moment, I'm able to give someone my new car—but I'm not willing. I'm able to give it away, but it's not going to happen, at least not today (smile).

Simply saying that God is able isn't a statement of faith, and faith is what pleases God (Hebrews 11:6). If you mishandle what you know to be true from the Word, that carelessness will hinder your harvest.

Let's continue with 2 Corinthians 9:9–11, "As it is written, He [the benevolent person] scatters abroad; He gives to the poor; His deeds of justice {and} goodness {and} kindness {and} benevolence will go on {and} endure forever! And [God] Who provides seed for the sower and bread for eating will also provide and multiply your [resources for] sowing and increase the fruits of your righteousness [which manifests itself in active goodness, kindness, and charity]. Thus you will be enriched in all things {and} in every way, so that you can be generous, and [your generosity as it is] administered by us will bring forth thanksgiving to God" (Ampl.).

When you give and disperse to the poor, your righteousness and good name will be remembered for eternity. Just think about Mother Teresa. No matter how much time has passed since she died, her good name and righteousness will be remembered forever—because people knew her to be a giver. You need to catch this—*your righteousness is your giving heart*. Knowing this, would you ever want to miss an opportunity to give? I wouldn't.

The point I'm driving home in your spirit is that you need to be careful to discern your seed for sowing versus your bread for eating. In other words, when God blesses you with money you have to learn how to seek Him to determine if it's been given to meet your need, or if you're supposed to help someone else and expect a harvest to come from it later. Let me restate one common sense way to discern quickly. Let's say that you've been praying for five thousand dollars in order to pay a bill and five hundred comes. **That's not the answer to your prayer, that's your seed.** Most people are careless and think, *I've got five hundred, so I can't pay the bill—but at least I can hold myself over until God answers my prayer*. Too many of God's people have missed out because when we receive something from Him, we don't pray about it; we just figure God is throwing us a temporary life raft...so we eat our seed.

Breakthrough won't come until you sow a seed, and God is willing to provide it for you so that you can plant it. God multiplies your seed sown, not your seed eaten. Sometimes you have to say, "Okay, God. You gave me five hundred dollars and this isn't enough to meet my need, so it must be a seed..." Then ask Him to direct you in giving. Make sure you find out which part is seed and which part is bread. God may not tell you to give the whole five hundred away; instead, He may tell you to take a certain amount from that five hundred to plant in the ground. Whatever God tells you to do...do it.

Turn It Over

Now, bear with me, because I'm going to tell you a story from when I used to be a drug dealer. We had something called *turnover*. Here's how it worked: When my partner and I were just starting and the others didn't really trust us, they'd only give us about an ounce of product at a time. After getting the product, we'd cut it with oregano (or whatever we needed to stretch the volume) and break it up into loose joints and bags before selling it. Let's say that we owed four hundred dollars for the product. By the time we cut it, broke it up into packages and sold it, we actually earned around fifteen hundred.

We could have said, "Ooh, after paying the four hundred, we've still got eleven hundred dollars. Whoop-tee-do!" and then spent every penny of it. Broke again, I would have had to go back and say, "Hook me one up one more time, man...I paid you before. I'll pay you again." I knew a lot of dealers who operated that way. But the smarter ones said, "Okay, I've got fifteen hundred; I'll pay four hundred, keep five hundred from this pack, and then buy the next pack with my own money. Next time, I'll get to keep all of the profit." That's what we did. We'd allocate a percentage of every purchase and keep turning our profit so that our next package could be bigger and more profitable.

This analogy may sound "thuggish," but I used it because the world has done too good a job of stealing the strategies of the kingdom. The devil has twisted the things that belong to God and used them in an evil world. That's why Jesus said in Luke 16:8 that the children of unrighteousness are wiser in this generation than the children of God. They've learned the same principles in the secular arena and have employed them in society...and it's working for them. Principles of high yields and returns have been created for God's children, but we've said, "No, I want to be humble. I don't want to ask for too much;

as long as I can feed my family and have enough to pay my bills, I'm satisfied." No! That's selfish...because when you think this way, you're thinking only about you and yours, and that's why you don't have what you desire.

You need to remain prayerful and recognize what God sends to meet your need versus what He gives you as a seed. Then when God blesses you, always look for an opportunity to turn that blessing over. Put some seed back in the ground so that you'll reap a more bountiful harvest next time. Remember the principle in Ecclesiastes 11:2, "Give a portion to seven, and also to eight..." Don't carelessly eat all of your seed; find out how much God wants you to give to others, and then start giving.

- 33 -

Guard Against Fear

Sowing sparingly because you fear that God might not get a harvest back to you on time will yield a small return. When you start receiving the blessings of God, especially when you're not used to having anything, it can make you want to hold on tight to them thinking, *I might not get this again*. Think about the poverty in that spirit. Think about the fear and demonic oppression in that spirit. God has blessed you, but you're holding onto it because He might not do it again? It's like saying, "I've got to count my eggs, Pastor; hold onto my basket...you know. I don't want to put all my eggs in one basket." Here's wisdom. If it's God's basket, put every one of your eggs into it.

Here's a personal story. My family had two cars: a 1988 Jeep Cherokee, which I used to bump around in the Poconos and a 2001 PT Cruiser, which became our main car. Whenever I took long road trips (because I didn't want to run up the mileage on our cars), I'd rent a car. I was being wise.

One day, I was asked to go to a service at my Bishop's church in Washington, D.C. The rental car dealership didn't have the car I usually drove, so we had to rent an economy car. I didn't really have a problem with it (except that it was small for my large frame). At the time, I was believing for my first luxury car. I sowed into it, brought it before the church, laid the receipt on the platform, and everybody prayed in agreement. God moved through me prophetically and I said, "Everybody who will agree with me is going to get your car." As time went by, everybody was coming to me with praise reports that they'd gotten their cars…only I still didn't have my car. To be honest, I was happy at first, but after a while it got a little tiring—watching everybody else get cars before I did.

The next time I was with my Bishop, he gave me a word, "By the way, son, on Monday you really need to go pick up that car." And I said, "Uh, I'm believing to pay for it cash; I have twenty-five hundred dollars so far…I don't think that's going to happen." He looked at me and said, "Son, this is the season you're in. You need to go get that car." Still intimidated, I said, "I can hear your intensity, and I know you're my man of God…I'm not closing you out; but help me to process this, because you're telling me to go and borrow the rest of the money…" He said, "Where you're called to go…" and continued giving me the word. But he could see that I was wrestling with the price tag, so he backed up and gave me breathing room.

As soon as I left him, I called the car dealership and said, "Here's my social security number…run the numbers; I'm coming in on Monday." I was still believing God to show up with the full amount by Monday; but in case He didn't, I settled within myself to obey the word of God through my man of God. This was difficult for me because I had done the same thing for members of the church. Someone would come to me and say, "I believe I'm supposed to quit my job." I'd say, "No, not yet…not in this season," and that person would have to choose to go against what he or she thought in order to obey what the man of God had said.

Up to that point, I'd never had somebody go against what I had heard from God, to instruct me. So I had to learn something new and overcome my fear of the unknown. The car dealership got back to me with a figure—and it was definitely a move of God. They were only asking for sixteen hundred dollars down on a forty thousand dollar car. I'd never heard of anything like that in my life. On top of that, they offered me 3.4 percent financing. Still, I was intimidated by the price tag. I wasn't able to see the blessing.

I went back to my Bishop and he said, "Wow, that's a good deal." When I told him how much it was going to cost me per month, he said, "Son, you don't need to get caught up in those numbers. You need to obey the word; because I'm telling you in my spirit, son, this is your season and you need to have that car…"

After our conversation, I called my Assistant Pastor and said, "What should I do? My man of God has mandated me to do this thing." And he said, "Well, when he asked you to pray about doing such-and-such event, from what I recall, you told him not to ask you to pray. If he believed that God wanted you to be there, the only thing he had to do was give you enough time to get packed. Didn't you say, 'Don't ask me to pray; just give me the instruction' "? Then he added, "What's the difference between that situation and the car?" "Well," I said, "If it was five hundred dollars a month, I'd be comfortable, but that eight something…" I wanted to pay what I had been used to paying, between three and four hundred dollars a month, while still being able to drive a luxury car.

That's the thing about being stretched. A lot of people get stretched, but they don't expand. God was stretching me, but I didn't want to give.

I got to the church on Sunday and sat down with my leaders. They had already met and talked. I told them, "Here's what I've been instructed to do. I'm going to go ahead and do this." Then they told me the news—they had taken up an offering for me, and it was about one-third of the ticket price! This was an amazing gesture, especially considering the members are primarily college students.

Because I had determined to obey God, I got the car of my desires and the payment ended up being what I was comfortable with…but He didn't show me how He was moving until I shook off the spirit of fear and said *Yes*. (See 2 Timothy 1:7.)

- 34 -

Guard Against Sowing in Unfertile Ground

When you sow your seeds in unfertile ground, your harvest will be unfruitful. This is what happened when the word was sown in stony or thorny ground in Mark 4:16–19. Remember, reaping a good harvest starts with plowing to make sure the ground is cleaned of impurities—but when you start scattering your seed, do you always make sure to know what kind of soil you're sowing into? Really consider this. God has put it on my heart to sow into certain ministries, and later He'd come to me in the Spirit when I was getting ready to sow again and cause me to lose that comfort level. I'd think, *I'm going to sow this seed because God told me to...* But the peace was gone.

Just because God moves in your heart to sow into a certain ministry doesn't mean that He wants you to support it forever. God might have been extending to them a season of grace, trying to get them to better their ways. And if they don't obey him, God will tell you, "Don't sow anymore." When this happens, you have to learn how to say, "I don't have a peace about it anymore." Peace should be the criteria, wherever and whenever you sow your seed. (See Philippians 4:6.) If I stood up in the pulpit and told people they weren't real Christians and were robbing God if they didn't pay tithes and offerings in this ministry, I'd be dead wrong.

Like I said before, compulsion and guilt are poor reasons to give. They should not be your motivation. Your motivation to give should come from a love and desire to be part of what God is doing. So if a church is making you feel guilty in order to force your giving, then you'd better think twice about sowing there—because you don't have any idea where your seed may be going. You'd might as well go outside and throw your seeds on the sidewalk.

The key is to make sure through prayer (i.e., receiving confirmation in your spirit) that you're sowing into the right soil. That way, when you see ministers on television or someplace else that are saying all of the right things—when you don't feel right in your spirit, you won't give them anything. There are people I watch every day on television who say, "If you're watching this ministry, you should be supporting it. If you're blessed by us, you should give us something."

That's when I go before God and ask, "Should I give them something?" Many times, God will say, "No, give it to *this* one." That could be the one you never see. "Give it to *him*," God will say, "That's where I'm telling you to give, not for the charming speeches." You have to sow by the Spirit if you're going to reap by the Spirit. Am I touching where you live? This is the way things work in God's economy. The Spirit of God must lead you when it comes to sowing your seed. That's when your harvest will be fruitful.

Also, make sure to be led by God about how much you sow. I've gotten to a point where I budget around what I want to sow for the year. I'm actually starting to take my budget and say, *How much do I want to give this year? How much do I need to take out of each check to get to that amount?* Then I begin to work my seed into my regular financial budget. I don't just go whimsically around sowing seeds, deciding at the last minute to give...I sit down with God and work it out, because the seeds that I sow are precious.

Try this for yourself. Sit down with God and say, "God, how much am I going to sow this year?" and He'll lead you by His Spirit. Then you can get your budget together and have everything ready. I'd even advise you to sit at home with your seed before giving at church on

Harvest Principle VI: Guard Against Losses

Sunday. Spend time with it. Minister to it...talk to God with your offering in your hands. Get intimate with your seed, because that's the crop you're going to reap.

Don't give out of guilt. Know what you're sowing by the Spirit. Look at ministries and see what they're doing for God. We had given regularly into a certain ministry. Then one day, God told me to send twenty bucks. "You can't do anything with twenty bucks," I said, "I want to send them more money." God said it again, "Send them twenty bucks." Afterwards, I received a couple of letters from them explaining their situation; and then the Lord revealed some things I needed to get in touch with them about. So I made a cassette tape and shared what God had put on my heart about why they weren't reaping the kind of harvest they desired.

Your financial seeds are precious. Know where you're going to sow and how much you're going to sow by the Spirit.

- 35 -

Guard Against Sowing in Unfavorable Conditions

Another reason you would receive a small harvest has to do with unfavorable conditions. Who creates the conditions in which you sow? According to Malachi 3, you do. If you're trying to reap a harvest and you're not getting enough sunshine or rain on your crops, then in some area, you're doing something incorrectly. Maybe you're not doing the right kind of bug extermination...and as simple as it sounds, in the natural realm an error in this area can destroy a harvest. How does this apply in the Spirit?

You can't control the rain or the sunshine. We've already covered this in Malachi 3. Let's look at this entire passage again:

> Even from the days of your fathers ye are gone away from mine ordinances, and have not kept *them*. Return unto me, and I will return unto you, saith the LORD of hosts. But ye said, Wherein shall we return? Will a man rob God? Yet ye have robbed me. But ye say, Wherein have we robbed thee? In tithes and offerings. Ye *are* cursed with a curse: for ye have robbed me, *even* this whole nation. Bring ye all the tithes into the storehouse, that there may be meat in mine house, and prove me now herewith, saith the LORD of hosts, if I will not open you the windows of heaven, and pour you out a blessing, that *there shall* not *be room* enough *to receive it*. And I will rebuke the devourer for your sakes, and he shall not destroy the

fruits of your ground; neither shall your vine cast her fruit before the time in the field, saith the LORD of hosts. And all nations shall call you blessed: for ye shall be a delightsome land, saith the LORD of hosts (vv. 7–12).

God cares about money. It's the only area where He allows us to test Him. This means, to guard against sowing into unfavorable conditions you must bring your tithe into the storehouse and prove the Lord…so that He'll do supernaturally what you cannot do in the natural.

Don't just bring your tithes into the storehouse…bring them with expectation. God has given some powerful promises in this scripture! If you bring your tithes to the storehouse reluctantly saying, "Okay, God, here it is…I'm going to watch to see if You're going to bless me," you have the wrong attitude! God said to *prove Him*…so you must come to the storehouse with some Holy Ghost gumption about you. "Dear Father, here it is…You promised me that You were going to open up the windows of heaven. So I'm going to sit right here and wait for You to tell me what's going on, because I know that You have a harvest for me…I gave you my check." God said, "Prove me…come on in here with some heart."

According to His Word, God will make your sowing conditions favorable. He'll rebuke the devourer for your sake so that your seeds won't fall to the ground before their time. And everybody, everywhere will look at your harvest and say how blessed you are. What an awesome promise! God will bless you so abundantly that everybody will see it. Joyfully give God what belongs to Him and your sowing conditions will be perfect.

Pray and Declare Your Harvest!

If you're faithfully giving your tithes and offerings, bow your head and pray with me.

"Father God, in the name of Jesus we understand that we've been tricked and deceived about the harvest. The devil has been telling us that You are our enemy, that You are against prosperity, and that You don't want us to enjoy abundance. But Your Word says that Your kindness leads us to repentance. So, Father, we seek You today for Your kindness. We ask You for wisdom, power, glory, and instruction."

Now, personalize it.

"Father God, if there's any way that I've let the enemy in, I say right now, rebuke the devourer on my behalf. I'm not going to waste my time fighting him, because he's already defeated. Instead, I'm going to keep my mind on Your provision. I'm going to focus on Your blessing. And I'm going to keep my mind on fellowship, love, peace, truth, and deliverance. Father, rebuke the devourer for me and protect my seed so that it doesn't fall to the ground before it's time. You've promised this in Your Word, so I believe, receive, and accept it. Right now, in the name of Jesus, I reverse the curse and receive everything that You've promised belongs to me."

Now, give God a shout of praise!

HARVEST PRINCIPLE VI
NINE WAYS TO GUARD AGAINST LOSSES

Don't Stop Planting Seeds
Lk. 6:38

Don't Be Impatient Once You've Planted
Gal. 6:7–9, Gen. 26:12, 2 Cor. 4:18

Don't Be Lazy and Fail to Reap
2 Tim. 4:2, Prov. 10:4

Don't Sow Sparingly
2 Cor. 9:6–10

Don't Be Selfish
Prov. 11:24, 2 Cor. 9:6, Acts 20:35, Rom. 12:8

Don't Be Careless with Your Seeds
2 Cor. 9:8–11, Heb. 11

Don't Be Fearful
2 Tim. 1:7

Don't Sow Seeds in Unfertile Ground
Mk. 4:16–19, Phil. 4:6

Don't Sow in Unfavorable Conditions
Mal. 3:7–12

Harvest Principle VII

Discern Your Harvest

- 36 -
Why One Hundredfold?

First Timothy 6:17 says, "Charge them that are rich in this world, that they be not highminded, nor trust in uncertain riches, but in the living God, who giveth us richly all things to enjoy…" There was a time when I didn't know that God provides richly for our enjoyment. Now, I know better, so I can no longer buy into the notion that God doesn't want His people to have anything of value in this life.

In Mark 10:17 the rich young ruler came to Jesus and asked, "…what must I do to inherit eternal life [that is, to partake of eternal salvation in the Messiah's kingdom]?" (Ampl.). Jesus said, "Keep My commandments; you know what they are" (Mark 10:19, paraphrased). That's just what he wanted to hear, because he was already keeping the Ten Commandments. Then Jesus added, "…You lack one thing; go and sell all you have and give [the money] to the poor…accompany Me [walking the same road that I walk]" (v. 21, Ampl.). With that, the rich young ruler got out of there. He went away disheartened because he possessed great riches.

Then Jesus looked at His disciples and said, "…With what difficulty will those who possess wealth {and} keep on holding it enter the kingdom of God….It is easier for a camel to go through the eye of a needle than for a rich man to enter the kingdom of God" (vv. 23, 25, Ampl.). Most people stop right there and say, "See…rich people can't go to heaven" because they're thinking, *There's no way you can get a camel through the eye of a needle.* Let's take a closer look at what Jesus really meant.

First of all, He wasn't talking about a sewing needle. If you were to visit a Middle Eastern country, you'd discover that the "needle" is a narrow opening in a mountain. In ancient times, many cities were built inside of mountains or walled fortresses. The small opening in the mountain was the location where they posted guards to make sure armies couldn't rush in on them.

Getting through the "eye of a needle" was a tedious process. Once the inhabitants reached the needle of the mountain, they had to get off of their camels and unload all of their belongings. Then they'd make the camel crouch down before leading it through the opening by rope. After that, they had to go back and drag all of their belongings through the needle, load them back onto the camel, and continue their journey. As you can see, going through the eye of a needle could be done, but it wasn't an easy process.

Harvest Principle VII: Discern Your Harvest

Knowing that Jesus wasn't talking about *impossibility* sheds a whole new light on this issue. When the Lord dealt with the rich young ruler, it wasn't because He didn't want him to have those riches; He just didn't want him to *trust in them*. You may have heard some religious people use this story to say, "Don't trust in riches, because God doesn't want you to be rich. He wants you to be poor." That's not at all what Jesus was saying, especially when you balance it with 1 Timothy 6:17. He was getting to the heart of that young man's issue, illustrating to him, "Don't trust in riches, but *trust in God* who gives us all things richly to enjoy." God doesn't have a problem with you having things and enjoying them.

This story goes on to say that the disciples were ASTONISHED. This puzzled me for a long time—because if the disciples were as poor and rag-tag as people make them out to be, why were they so astonished? It seems to me they would have said, "Well, no problem, we don't have anything anyway." But they were astonished and said amongst themselves, "Well then, who can go to heaven?" **Poor men wouldn't ask this question.**

The story continued, "Jesus glanced around at them and said, With men [it is] impossible, but not with God; for all things are possible with God. Peter started to say to Him, Behold, we have yielded up and abandoned everything....Jesus said, Truly I tell you, there is no one who has given up and left house or brothers or sisters or mother or father or children or lands for My sake and for the Gospel's who will not receive a hundred times as much **NOW IN THIS TIME**—houses and brothers and sisters and mothers and children and lands, with persecutions—and in the age to come, eternal life" (Mark 10:27–30, Ampl., emphasis added).

Do you see this? Jesus wasn't telling His men to take a vow of poverty. Instead, He was saying, "Relinquish the earth's system of prosperity and get into My system." He was trying to teach them a powerful principle. If the rich young ruler had done what Jesus instructed him to do, he would have gotten back A HUNDRED TIMES more possessions than what he had sold!

Think about it. We read this scripture and think it's saying, "Sow to the poor, then you will have treasure in heaven...because you can't ever have it again until you die." No! Jesus didn't say that, and neither did Timothy. First Timothy 6:17 tells us not to trust in *uncertain riches*, but to trust in God and receive a return in this life."

In case you're thinking, *Pastor, I'm not rich; so what does that have to do with me?* Let me tell you something. You don't have to be rich according to the world's standards to have a problem with trusting in riches. A lot of poor people trust in their "riches." For example, you may not be rich, but you could be trusting in a job, a family member, or some other person as your source. Telltale thinking like, *Oh, if she doesn't help me out, I'm not going to be able to get this loan*...will tell you where your heart is. You don't have to have a lot of possessions to fall into the trap of trusting in the resources you currently have.

Here's a true story that illustrates my point. It happened when I was a new Christian; so I had a lot of zeal, but not a lot of wisdom. One day, I saw a homeless man on the street that had a shopping cart full of junk. He smelled terrible, his cart stunk, and his shoes were bursting out at the seams. I walked over to him and started talking to him about Jesus Christ.

Afterwards, trying to be a good Christian and have pity on the poor, I went home, pulled together some nice clothes and shoes (new things that I'd just purchased from The Gap), and took it all back to the homeless man. I gave him the bag of clothing items and twenty dollars, which was worth more than everything he had in his cart. Then I invited him to come home with me so that I could clean him up. Weeping, he said: "I can't go with you because if I leave, somebody will steal my cart."

I was amazed. So I asked him, "What's in your cart that's worth more than the twenty dollars I just gave you? I'll even buy the cart from you." You see, that cart was his worldly treasure. He wasn't interested in going to heaven if he couldn't take that cart with him. This poor man was trusting in his riches! You don't have to be the wealthiest person in the world to trust in material things. Do you see my point? Many people lay hold of material things and make *things* their source, instead of laying treasure up in heaven (regardless of its earthly value), where they'll have wealth to draw on when they need it.

Remember, if you give God *all of you*, He'll give you all of Himself. Stop thinking: *God gives me just enough to get by, so I won't ask for too much; He knows I don't have need of that.* God isn't holding out on you. He's not stingy. So fight the "good fight" of faith according to 1 Timothy 6:12, knowing that God gives you all things richly to enjoy.

- 37 -
How Big is the Harvest?

In Chapter 21, we reviewed Ecclesiastes 11:1–3 that says a tree falls where it's going to be—whether it's north, south, east, or west. In

Harvest Principle VII: Discern Your Harvest

other words, it lands where it lands. During this process, along with discerning your seed, you must also discern the size of your harvest before going to get it. God tells us to sow our seed and divide it out, because it's going to come back…but it isn't just going to land in our hands. The harvest is going to fall, and when it does, are you going to stand there singing, "Kumbaya" or are you going to get out there and reap your harvest?

Again, I believe Christians have been thinking that harvest is automatic. It's not this way in the natural world, and guess what, it's not like that in the Spirit realm either. By and large, we have to locate our harvest and gather it.

This is why it's vitally important to discern the difference between a blessing and a miracle, because like I said before, God doesn't want us to live from miracle to miracle. He doesn't want us to get into such a mess financially that He has to suspend the natural laws in order to deliver us. I've heard people saying things like, "I was praying and praying, because I knew God could do it, and one day I just opened my Bible and there was my rent money."

Don't misunderstand me, God can and will do things like that for you under extreme circumstances, but allow me to point this out again. That's not how you're supposed to live! As a people of God, we're supposed to be actively involved with God…working with Him in seedtime and in harvest. In doing so, God promised that He'd bless everything we put our hands to. (See Deuteronomy 28.) This means if we don't put our hands to *something*, then God doesn't have *anything* to bless. This is pretty simple.

I remember once being offered a deal and I didn't know if I wanted to do it, so I prayed and asked God, "Should I get into this? God, I'm waiting on you." (I was believing and claiming—"If it's Your will, Lord, if it's Your will…") God finally said to me, "I'll bless whatever you put your hands to that's in line with My Word. You're quoting scriptures every day, but if you don't put your hands to something, I won't have anything to bless."

In the book of Genesis, God told Adam to go forth and name every beast of the field and every fowl of the air (2:19–20). God wants us to participate with Him. That's why He said in Isaiah 1:18, "Come now, and let us reason together…" The choice is ours, because God wants us to partner with Him. Living from miracle to miracle is not what God intended for His children.

You must discern the harvest (from your acts of faith in partnership with God) and then go out and reap it. And remember, you won't reap a great harvest if you fail to discern how big it actually is. Let me explain. Let's say you were to plant a field, and then went out at harvest time with a picnic basket gathering up everything your faith could muster—this would reflect what you believed that you deserved to receive from God (because, after all, you know that you have to be humble, right?). Then you'd fill up your little basket and return home (tra-la-la-la-la), leaving the remaining crops in the field.

Think about it. Have you ever been guilty of doing this? Here's the bottom line: You decide the amount that you sow, and you determine the amount that you reap. You choose whether you get a little or a lot.

You could have heard different analogies all of your life, things like, "You have to accept the hand you've been dealt," or, "You've got a good job over there, you'd better shut up and just stay there because you're going to get great benefits when you retire." So you stayed somewhere that was out of the will of God for your life for another twenty-five years just to receive retirement benefits. (I'm not saying that you shouldn't be responsible; I'm saying that any one of us can settle for less than the best if we're not careful. Think about how Esau sold his birthright in Genesis 25:29–34 for a plate of food when he was hungry…the stew was right in front of him, looking and smelling delicious, but it wasn't God's best. Esau failed to discern the greatness of his harvest.)

Let's be realistic. When you work as an employee, the company offers you ten or twenty thousand dollars less in pay to give you benefits and a 401K. People who have witnessed my entrepreneurial pursuits have asked me, "What are you going to do if someone in your family gets sick?" I always tell them; "I'm going to pay for it out of my fat bank account." Now, if you're working for low pay so that you can get benefits, you probably don't have this type of liquidity. In other words, you don't have a lot of cash in the bank. Personally, I'm not working to get sick. And I'm not planning to put my family members in the hospital.

These so-called benefits that companies offer aren't always what they seem to be. If you die, your wife might get a note saying, "We're so sorry to hear about your loss…" along with a bouquet of flowers. Trust me; there are other ways to protect your family than what is common for employees in the corporate world.

Ask yourself these questions and take them before God: *What am I going to bring in? Where am I going to find it, and how much will there be?* Discern your harvest and then go get it.

Harvest Principle VII: Discern Your Harvest

- 38 -
Is it Time to Reap?

Another thing you need to discern is when it's time to gather your harvest. In other words, is your harvest ready now, or will it be ripe later? Let's go to John 4:35, "Say not ye [don't say], There are yet four months, and then cometh harvest? behold, I say unto you, Lift up your eyes, and look on the fields; for they are white already to harvest."

Jesus was talking about souls in this passage, but I believe it applies to every area of the kingdom because the principles of harvesting are consistent. Jesus said, "Look around you. The fields are white unto the harvest. Don't say it's not harvest time right now." Have you been saying it isn't time to reap? If so, *according to your faith*, it will be unto you...even if you've plowed, set the environment, and planted. The church is famous for saying, "It's not time" when the opposite is true.

Let me bring this into practical terms. Unsaved people are prospering all over the world. So why are Christians still saying, "At a certain time, we're going to do something..." or, "I know that things are going to get better one day, but this isn't the time right now to build a church." Why do Christians feel this way when the unsaved are building gigantic skyscrapers every day?

Don't say that it's not harvest time. It is time, now. The fields are ready to be reaped. Jesus is saying, "Go reap them"...and you should heed this, especially if you've plowed and planted in the right environment. Now, let's go back to John 4:35. Again, Jesus is saying, "Don't say four more months and then I'll have a harvest, for the fields are ready now" (paraphrased). What does this really mean? The harvest is available now, though you might not see it with the natural eye...it's white...it's spiritual.

God has to make your heart ready to receive a harvest before He can get you to reap it. As I said before, He isn't going to take your "poverty spirit" and bless you with millions of dollars because in a little while you'll be broke again. You'll gravitate back toward what you perceive yourself to be. **God is saying there's a time to reap, but you have to reap in the Spirit first.**

Let me make it clear and simple. This is why you have to get to the place where you stop saying, "It's not time." You can't do this in the flesh. It can only be done through staying in the Word and in prayer. When you get to the place where you can actually see that the harvest is yours (that Jesus paid for it two thousand years ago, and you're tenacious enough to jump out there and go for it where God's Spirit is leading you—be it to the north, south, east, or west), then He can open the doors for you to go forward in the natural as you follow His direction. Your perspective must change first.

Motivational speakers and teachers say that perspective is everything. *How big do you see yourself as being?* Remember, when Joshua and Caleb were trying to get the Israelites to go into the Promised Land, the other ten spies were saying, "...we were in our own sight as grasshoppers, and so we were in their sight" (Numbers 13:33, Ampl.). This was their perspective. They really didn't know how the "giant" people saw them...they were sneaking and peeking around in the bushes. So in reality, the enemy didn't see them at all. The ten spies saw themselves that way, and because of this, the devil made sure the Israelites embraced that perspective.

The same is true when we experience doubts or fears. The devil will make sure that somebody comes along to say, "Oh, you want to go there? You don't want to go there. You don't really want to do that." And we accept those negative reports...hook, line, and sinker, "Watch out, brother, because the last person who went to that school lost all of his money; the school didn't even give him a diploma. And beyond that, three students got killed there in a fire." The enemy will give you every reason why you shouldn't pursue your harvest, but he can only succeed if you see yourself from a "grasshopper" perspective.

Now, let's move on. Psalm 126 says, "When the Lord brought back the captives [who returned] to Zion, we were like those who dream [it seemed so unreal]. Then were our mouths filled with laughter, and our tongues with singing. Then they said among the nations, The Lord has done great things for them. The Lord has done great things for us! We are glad! Turn to freedom our captivity *and* restore our fortunes [not our paychecks], O Lord, as the streams in the South (the Negeb) [are restored by the torrents]" (vv. 1–4, Ampl., emphasis added).

This scripture clearly states that God wants His people to prosper and bring in a harvest. Give close attention to the next two verses, "They who sow in tears shall reap in joy *and* singing. He who goes forth bearing seed and weeping [at needing his precious supply of grain for sowing] shall doubtless come again with rejoicing, bringing his sheaves [or his harvest] with him" (vv. 5–6, emphasis added).

God is saying, "Sow, even if you have to cry, if you have to dig down in the bottom of the pot..." I was there; I did a lot of crying. But

Harvest Principle VII: Discern Your Harvest

I kept sowing. One woman we know used to make fun of me when I was in my sowing and crying season. She'd say, "How are you paying that low rent? How is your tithing?" Now, I'm not crying anymore. I'm reaping and laughing—because this principle works.

When God brings you out of bondage into a place of blessing; it seems so unreal, it's like a dream. When we moved into our first home, I often looked out of my upstairs window. There was a little windowshade that was shaped like a stop sign...it reminded me of the portals in a boat. I'd swing that little window open just to look outside at nature. When the grass and trees were beginning to flourish, it was so beautiful. Then sometimes I'd glance down and marvel at our two cars sitting in the driveway.

During those times when I looked out upon my harvest, something would happen inside of me. Driving home from work at night, I'd see the trees and experience that fresh smell of our new surroundings...and the feeling was almost indescribable. You see, I was born and raised in the ghetto, so the beauty of nature was (and still is) exciting to me. People who are used to being in a scenic environment might not appreciate it like I do; because to them, it's common. For me, it's heaven. For me, it's like a dream.

Often during my time of struggle, I stood on Psalm 126. I'd say, "God, when You bring me in, it's going to be like a dream." I stood on that word and it gave me strength. I'd say, "I'm sowing now, weeping, but one day I'm going to reap in joy and laughter."

No matter where you are financially at this moment, I hope this encourages you. You will reap if you don't faint, and when you do, you'll be reaping with joy and laughter. Stop and declare right now, "I'm discerning my harvest. It's out there, and I'm going to bring it in at just the right time."

- 39 -

Where is the Harvest?

Where is the harvest? North? South? East? West? Let's go to Luke 5, "And it came to pass, that, as the people pressed upon him to hear the word of God, he stood by the lake of Gennesaret, and saw two ships standing by the lake: but the fishermen were gone out of them, and were washing their nets. And he entered into one of the ships, which was Simon's, and prayed him that he would thrust out a little from the land. And he sat down, and taught the people out of the ship" (vv. 1–3).

Harvest Time: What's That All About?

You've probably heard this story. Jesus approached Peter and the other fishermen while they were washing their nets. I want to make sure you get the picture—they weren't fishing with poles or rods and reels. They were commercial fishermen; they fished for a living, so they had to use big nets to haul in a huge catch of fish at one time. At the end of a workday, they weren't just cleaning seaweed off of a line and a hook. They weren't taking little worms and putting them back into a container. Their nets were huge—so they had a big, tedious cleaning job on their hands once fishing was done. That's when Jesus came.

After they had packed everything away, Jesus walked up to them and said, "I want to use your boat to preach a sermon." Now, think about it. They didn't know Him as Lord. This stranger (with a crowd behind Him) just walked up and said, "Let me use your boat to preach." These guys had been out fishing all night, but they still obeyed His word. Then Jesus told them to put down their nets for a catch. That's when Peter said, "We've been fishing all night. We haven't caught anything" (vv. 4–5). He probably wanted to add, "We're tired and want to go home."

Keith Moore once said, "God is not a moocher." The Lord isn't a bum. The best thing you could ever do is to let God use you or your "stuff." If God tells you to give your coat, shoes, car, or anything else to somebody in need, the best thing you could possibly do is to let Jesus use it. This is part of the harvesting process.

So in actuality, Peter and the other fishermen sowed into Jesus' ministry the moment that Peter allowed Him to use his boat and they all decided to stay with Him while He taught. When Jesus told them to put down their nets for a catch, that was their harvest. If you've read through this story in Luke 5, you'll remember that at first, Peter wasn't excited about doing this. Nevertheless, he said, "...on the ground of Your word, I will lower the nets [again]" (v. 5, Ampl.).

These men were professionals; they knew that it was best to go fishing at night—yet it was daybreak. Technically, they knew that no fish would be in the water, because when the sun comes out, the fish go down. Not on that day—not when they had obeyed the voice of the Lord. They threw in the nets and caught so many fish that the nets were about to break. So they yelled to the other fishermen on shore, "Come on...help us get this stuff in!" And they filled up both of the boats, until the boats began to sink (vv. 6–7).

Let's think about this. When Jesus told Peter and the others to drop their nets, they were reluctant to do it at first—but when they did,

Harvest Principle VII: Discern Your Harvest

they caught such a harvest the boats almost went underwater. Other fishermen had to come from the shore to help catch some of the surplus. Make the comparison. Where is your harvest? What has Jesus told you to do?

Wherever Jesus tells you to drop your net, that's where your harvest will be. Many people miss their harvest for fear of letting go of those things they've become accustomed to. Lowering the nets didn't seem to be the right thing for them to do...especially after cleaning them from the night before and knowing that it was daybreak. If Jesus is telling you to thrust out on the water and cast your nets, why are you hanging on to them? If He tells you to make a move, would you say, "Well, I have to stay here for my pension..."? What you're thinking may seem to be right, but again, if Jesus is leading you somewhere else, I don't think staying is the wise thing to do.

Jesus was saying to the fishermen, "No, go over there. *That's the harvest.*" Peter was reluctant at first, but when he and the others dropped the nets, they were so overwhelmed that they had to give some of the blessings to others just to keep Peter's boat from sinking. That's powerful. If you want to know where your harvest is, it's where Jesus says, "Drop the net."

Have you ever felt like you should do something, but when you asked a lot of people about it, they told you, "No, you can't...you shouldn't"? Then later, you looked back and realized, *I could have been part of something great.* (Let me help you by being plain; this means you could have taken advantage of an excellent opportunity, and you didn't.) When Jesus tells you where to find your harvest, you'll have a knowing in your spirit that you need to drop the net on another side. This means He may tell you to pursue another area you otherwise wouldn't have thought about; something you aren't used to: something out of the ordinary.

I've got news for you. If you keep painting a house with white paint, you can fast and pray all you want; it's not going to turn blue. You have to go to the store and pick up a different color. You can't buy what you've always used if you want something more colorful or of a better quality.

On the other hand, let's say that you buy the paint and then start throwing it on the wall: fast, slow, then at medium speed—thinking, *Maybe if I just keep doing this, eventually the finish will be right.* No! You're beating at the air without aim..., which is what happens when you venture out without Jesus. Have you ever been guilty of this?

I've heard the saying, "If you stay down, you have to come up." That's not true. I used to stay down, and I never came up...until I realized something. If you want to go up, you have to get on the stairs, the elevator, or climb up a ladder. You have to go to a different place and do something different. Say this and mean it, "I have to go somewhere different and do something different to reap a different result." Change is scary to the natural man. When you're used to something working a certain way (even if it hasn't been favorable), you tend to stick with it until you get your break. No! What you're going to do is break your back, because if it didn't work before, it's not going to work now.

You have to change where you are and what you're doing to see something different in the future. Jesus won't ever lead you to do something that won't yield fruit—but like everyone else, you can probably be stubborn. You may not want to throw your nets on *that* side of the boat because you're thinking, *There aren't any fish over there.* So you'll resist the Holy Spirit and say, "Everybody told me they won't be there; all of my relatives, everybody." But He'll keep saying, "If you want to serve Me, let Me use your life. Let Me borrow your boat, and I'll bless you…step this way."

Once you learn to drop your nets for a catch, you'll not only get a harvest every time, but you'll experience amazing supernatural joy. Joy always bubbles up within you during harvest time, even though you can't begin to explain why. Suddenly, you just feel good all over. You get excited, *Oh, yeah. Things are starting to happen now. I don't know what it is...but something's getting ready to happen!*

Let me illustrate with a story. You go to your spouse and say, "Honey, I don't know why, but I'm just feeling a strong thing about a car…" and then you start describing it. Of course, the devil will immediately try to tell you, "You can't do that. How are you going to pay for that? You'd better start with a used car." Then the phone rings fifteen minutes later with a relative who quips, "You…get a new car?" Suddenly, you don't want that car anymore, so you rationalize, *For the kind of traveling I'm going to be doing, I only need an old car. The city streets will mess up my new car anyway.* Right away, somebody's always there trying to talk you out of believing what God is doing…this minimizes the blessing you are able to reap.

You have to have the supernatural sense to say, "I'm dropping my net on the other side." The joy in your spirit will confirm it! If you sow in joy, you'll reap in joy. Joy confirms the word of the Lord about where to find your blessing. A member of our church called me once and said, "Pastor, I don't know why, but I'm going to move to Connecticut.

I'm packing all of my stuff. I'm ready to go..." And He was ready to go! He was ready to drop it all and go at the word of the Lord. I got excited about that, because I knew he was ready...yet, the Lord told me to counsel him, "Just slow down a little bit."

Actually, he shared that he was calling me to get confirmation, because those "enemies" had already started giving him every reason why he couldn't do it. I bore witness that God had already given him the "go." While we were still talking, he said, "I'm hanging up, I'm straight. Bye." The joy returned to him and that gave him peace to do what was in his spirit. He knew it was God. All of the natural circumstances didn't make sense, but he had peace and joy about it, so he followed Jesus step by step...and God blessed him mightily.

When you hear the word of the Lord and experience that supernatural joy, go with it. Move out on what God tells you to do. He knows exactly where the harvest is. Remember, you can't steer a parked car and you can't use it to get where you're going. When Jesus speaks, move at His Word.

- 40 -

How Much Can You Reap?

How much of the harvest can you have? Let's go back to the book of Numbers and look at chapter 14, after Joshua and Caleb had brought a good report about the Promised Land and the other spies reported the opposite. All of the congregation wept that night because they believed the false report. Then the story continues:

> Then Moses and Aaron fell on their faces before the assembly of the congregation of the children of Israel. And Joshua the son of Nun, and Caleb the son of Jephunneh, *which were* of them that searched the land, rent their clothes: And they spake unto all the company of the children of Israel, saying, The land, which we passed through to search it, *is* an exceeding good land. If the Lord delight in us, then he will bring us into this land, and give it us; a land which floweth with milk and honey. Only rebel not ye against the Lord, neither fear ye the people of the land; for they are bread for us: their defence is departed from them, and the Lord *is* with us: fear them not (vv. 5–9).

In other words, don't tempt God. If He says you can do it, go and take the land. Keep in mind, the other men had already said, "We can't do it. It's not going to happen. Not today. We don't have the power...these people are like giants; they're going to kill us all. Can we just forget about this and go home?" And that's exactly what they did...the whole tribe of Israel.

Harvest Time: What's That All About?

Joshua and Caleb were grieved in their hearts, so they kept trying to convince the people, "Listen, we can do this thing. Let's go in and take the land. Let's go do this." Then verse ten says, "But all the congregation bade stone them with stones..." The Israelites wanted to kill Joshua and Caleb because they didn't have enough confidence in God to take the land, even with a sample of the harvest already in their hands; because Joshua and Caleb had brought back some of the fruits from Canaan and laid them before their very eyes.

Like I said before, when you make a decision to go and take the land, many people will want to shoot you down. I find it interesting that a lot of poor preachers (who can't pay their bills) always have something bad to say about the faith preachers who can. This amazes me. They don't have anything, but they're speaking against the ones who are on television thrusting out into the deep for a catch. Every day, these ministers are reaching the world for God, traveling in their own jets—and some angry preacher in a little storefront church is declaring how the others aren't right, and how their lifestyle isn't of God.

One day, something occurred to me. I thought, *Look at how God's blessing them. Maybe somebody needs to tell God that these ministers have the wrong message.* It's ludicrous! God's taking good care of them, so I don't understand those who say that "prosperity preachers" are wrong. Because at the same time these people are accusing others, their testimony is filled with poverty, lack, sickness, dissension in the church, and so on. Yet, the prosperity preachers are supposed to be phonies and hypocrites! If so, how are so many experiencing clear manifestations of God?

Joshua and Caleb were trying to show the people the fat of the land, and in response, they wanted to kill them both—but that didn't matter to Joshua, because he knew God had told Moses they would possess the land. You know the story. That whole generation died without entering the Promised Land...except for Joshua and Caleb. God said to Joshua, "Moses my servant is dead; now therefore arise, go over this Jordan, thou, and all the people....Be strong and of a good courage: for unto this people [not the ones who didn't believe] shalt thou divide for an inheritance the land, which I sware unto their fathers to give them" (Joshua 1:2 and 6, emphasis added).

How much can you reap? How much are you willing to possess? Look at Joshua's story. Don't make the mistake of deciding the task is too great and, therefore, conclude that you can't do what God has told you to do. How much can you believe the word of the Lord in your life? A little? Then you'll reap a small harvest. A lot? Your harvest will be great.

- 41 -
Don't Sleep through Your Harvest

Proverbs 10:5 says, "He who gathers in the summer is a wise son: but he that sleepeth in harvest is a son that causeth shame." The first implication of this scripture reveals that there is a process of gathering during harvest time. In other words, it's possible to sleep through your harvest. If you're not awake and alert, you can miss it. There was a time I didn't understand this. I thought in order to get my harvest, I had to pray, sow, confess...and then it would just come. As I've said before, this isn't how it works on a farm. Crops can't jump up out of the ground (or off of the branch) and run into the barn by themselves!

You can't just confess it, claim it in the name of Jesus, and then wake up one day to find a package resting in your hands. Do you want to be a wise or foolish son (or daughter)? I had to decide that I wanted to be wise. I didn't want to sleep through my hour of opportunity. In other words, I had to recognize that when God presented an opportunity, I needed to move forward on it in order to prosper. If I didn't seize the opportunity, I wouldn't reap.

Let me share a personal experience. God blessed me with my own business in 1995, a management production company. As it started to move forward, I got a record production contract with a major label and some of my other clients were cast in one of the *Die Hard* movies. What a wonderful time that was! Then suddenly, the business started getting slower and slower. Nevertheless, I still kept my office, confessing, fasting, and so on. I read my Bible, prayed, prayed, and prayed some more—but nothing changed. All of this happened in one year.

I didn't want to let my business go because I didn't want to fail. As a result, I wasn't praying, "God, are You moving me into something else right now? Is there somewhere else I need to be? Is there another harvest that I need to be looking into during this season?" No! I was trying to make fruit come out of dead ground. You see, sometimes you have to release what isn't producing and move on. But we get stuck into thinking, *This is the way God blessed me last time, so He has to bless me the same way this time*, **and we hold on to something that is no longer under the anointing.** God was trying to tell me *where*, and I was in a spiritual stupor—I was sleeping through my harvest!

Jesus told Nicodemus in John 3:8, "The wind bloweth where it listeth, and thou hearest the sound thereof, but canst not tell whence it cometh, and whither it goeth…" describing those who are led by the Holy Spirit. When I read this passage, God revealed to me that we have to be like spiritual sailboats. When the wind blows to the right, we just flow over there with Him; and when He blows to the left, we flow to the left. We should always go where the Holy Spirit goes, because that's where our harvest is going to be. Don't sleep through your harvest, saying, "Well, I've been on this job and I've been believing for a promotion." Maybe God doesn't want to promote you on that job; maybe He wants to promote you somewhere else. Be obedient to the voice of the Lord.

Finally, God spoke to my heart and said, "It's time to let this office go. I blessed you in it, I prospered you in it, and now you're losing your blessing trying to keep it—because you're paying money for something that's not supporting itself. Turn it loose." It took me six more months to do it. I was still praying, trying to get God to change His mind and bless the office I had grown used to. He was finished there. Ultimately, I stopped praying for God to fix what I was doing and said, "God, what are You trying to do right now?" Are you at that place? Is this what you need to hear to let go and let God?

After I said, "Okay, God, where do I need to be?" a minister in my church called and gave me a word, "Step out, pick something." So I went before God and told Him I wanted to go into computer networks, because when I prayed, I really felt like I heard that in my spirit. But when this blessing came, I took it as a step down because it wasn't my own business. Why would God tell me to go take a computer job or direct me to go after another career? Yet, I knew God had put the word "computer" in my heart. When I prayed, I didn't know what a computer job was worth. Even more amazing was the fact that I had no network skills, so I didn't think it was possible for me to get into that occupation. God knew for that season there would be plenty of income for me in computers, so He placed me there.

You have to be alert in order to discern. The disciples kept falling asleep on Jesus in the Garden of Gethsemane; therefore, when the soldiers came and arrested Jesus, they were stupefied. It didn't have to be that way—He kept telling them to "watch and pray," but they didn't. (See Matthew 26:36–41.) God has always prospered and blessed me when I've stepped out on His Word—so whenever He tells me it's time to leave something, I do it. Now, I go wherever He tells me to go and He blesses me. When I followed Him in pursuing my career, I took a job getting paid less, but before I left I was making four times more than I'd earned previously.

Harvest Principle VII: Discern Your Harvest

You must be alert and available during the harvesting season so that you'll be able to go into the harvesting field in the right timing and reap. What would have happened if I had just sat in my office and prayed for a computer job? I'd still be starving. I had to do *something*. For one thing, I had to make up a resume. (When I look at that resume now, I laugh, because it's pitiful—it's the most awful resume that I've ever seen. Nobody should have given me a job, but because I was obedient to put my resume out there God used it to bless me.)

That's not all I did. I went on the Internet and found the fax number of every possible placement company and faxed that resume to about twenty-five people. Then I went over to the college I used to attend and told them that I needed a job. I went out into the field and sowed my seed so that I could take the land. Some people would say, "No, brother, you just need to wait on God." Let me clear something up for you. Waiting on the Lord is an active word; it doesn't mean that you should sit back and do nothing (see Psalm 27:14/Strong's 6960). I had to get out there and put something in the ground, so that when harvest time came, I could reap something. Waiting on the Lord isn't just sitting at home praying. It's watching for Him in earnest expectation.

Here's another analogy. Let's say somebody at a convention walked up to the podium, flashed a set of keys to a new Mercedes Benz and said, "There's a parking lot at the mall in New Jersey with a brand new Benz in it and God said to tell you it's yours." Do you think everybody would get on their knees and pray, "Oh, Lord, lead me to the car...show me the way, Lord"? Then if they still didn't hear anything, would they pray, fast, and cry out, "Oh, Lord, why haven't You shown me where to find the car? Oops...sorry Lord; I didn't mean to confess that. I believe it, I receive it, Lord. It's mine..."

Here's what I'd do. While everybody else was going through that process, I would have taken the keys, gone to every mall in New Jersey and started putting them in the door of every Mercedes Benz that I could find until one of them opened up. "This one's mine," I'd say. *Don't sleep through your harvest!* If you leave that Mercedes there long enough, it's going to get ticketed for being illegally parked and be towed away. I don't know about you, but when God gives me a word...I'm going into the harvest field.

When the plowing is done, the environment is set, and you've sown your seeds—it's time to reap. Don't skip plowing and tithing, and then go out into the field expecting to reap a godly harvest. Proverbs

10:4 says, "He becometh poor that dealeth *with* a slack hand: but the hand of the diligent maketh rich." This verse comes right before, "He that gathereth in the summer is a wise son: *but* he that sleepeth in harvest..." (v. 5). Some people walk around saying, "See, Pastor, when the Lord is ready, He'll show up." When I hear this, I say, "Maybe the Lord did show up, but you slept through it."

Listen to me. Time does pass between sowing and reaping, but it doesn't take God fifteen years to get something back to you. When God merely gives you an unction in your spirit, He's letting you sense a coming season; but if a prophet lays hands on you and prophesies, "You're in the season now...it's time," then it's a *right now* word. The Lord is setting something up. If you take three years to reap this blessing, something's wrong on your end.

God doesn't send His prophet to give you a *right now* word if He doesn't mean for it to happen quickly. It should not take years for a *right now* word to come to pass. If so, here's what will happen. You'll start saying, "He didn't speak the right word over me; I don't know if that's what God really said..." If you go to sleep spiritually after receiving a *right now* word, you'll start to question whether or not the prophet (who you should know to actually be a true prophet) heard correctly. Most likely, the prophet did hear God accurately...but you were asleep. Remember: If you sleep through your harvest, you'll miss your appointed time.

Has anyone ever approached you and confirmed something that was on your heart, and you said, "Yes, I bear witness with what the Lord is speaking through you"? Initially, you got excited, but then you didn't go forward based on the excitement that God put in your spirit. You went and asked some of your loser friends and family (the ones with no godly vision) for their opinions. And they said, "Well, it sounds good, but maybe what the Lord really means is this..." That ungodly counsel got you off track, so you kept asking different people and getting more and more confused until you could finally find somebody that agreed with your foolishness. Do you see the poverty in that spirit?

The problem with people that have mastered poverty or lack is they bring a rich harvest back to the lack they've become accustomed to. The poverty in their spirit despises the wealth that's trying to come in...because poverty is repulsed by wealth. Therefore, people will say that they want to have wealth, but because poverty is still in them they'll put ten thousand dollars in their bank account and turn it into two hundred fifty making stupid purchases—because the bank balance has to get back down to the same level as their spirit of poverty. That's why God won't put wealth in just anybody's hands.

If you haven't allowed God to deal with the poverty inside of you, it won't make a difference what He puts in your hands, because you're going to take it back to where you're comfortable. Read the stories about the Lotto millionaires and where they are today. You'll find if they were poor before they won the money, they were soon poor again. If they were rich before they got it, they became richer. The poor slept through their harvest—the rich stayed alert and maximized their blessing.

- 42 -

Go In and Possess

Let's go back to Joshua and Caleb. The twelve spies went into Canaan and saw the land of giants. Ten of them punked out and said, "We can't take the land." Remember, God had already told them the land belonged to them. It was flowing with milk and honey and had grapes the size of grapefruits. I could really enjoy a place like that! Joshua and Caleb "rent their clothes" and pleaded with the others to believe and move forward. But, as you know, that generation didn't believe God, nor did they possess the land.

Let's review. When it comes to bringing in the harvest, who is responsible to bring it in? *We are.* The other spies were telling Joshua all the reasons why they couldn't go in and possess Canaan. Remember, the person who waits for favorable conditions will not sow and the one who regards the clouds will not reap (Ecclesiastes 11:4). Israel had run into unfavorable conditions. While considering these conditions, **they decided** that they wouldn't reap. And Joshua kept urging them, "Listen…God said we could do it; *let's do it.*" Instead of rising up in faith, they wanted to kill those who had vision.

That's heavy. Why did the people want to kill them? I think it's because God was using Joshua and Caleb to bring conviction that the Israelites were not moving forward to possess what rightfully belonged to them. The same thing happens today. In fact, many ministers who have declared to the body of Christ that we can take what belongs to us have been stoned. This happens when people say things like, "Oh, that's a cult…they're demonic…" Do you see how easily we can fall into the same pattern of error that stopped an unbelieving generation from inheriting God's promises?

Joshua and Caleb's generation had been in the wilderness for forty years because of their lack of faith in God. After they wouldn't move forward, God said to them (and I'm paraphrasing), "You're all going to die in the wilderness...the only people I'm going to let go into the Promised Land is the younger generation." Joshua and Caleb were not of the younger generation, but they were the only two who said, "We can take the land." So God said, "The young kids and the two of you are going in."

To me, when you refuse to grow in the Lord, you're dead. When you've decided that you've done all that you can do, and you can't do any more than that...you're dead right then. The first generation of Israelites died before their time—because they didn't believe they could become what God had destined them to be. I know people in their eighties and nineties who are vibrant, living, going forth in God, taking the land...and doing much better than many of the younger "old people" that I know. You know the type—sitting around, "confessing" and talking, but all the while doing nothing.

After waiting forty years for the "old people" to die off, Joshua and Caleb were blessed to lead the second generation. Think about it. They waited forty years to begin receiving the promise they were willing to reap when they first saw the land. The unbelievers said, "Shut them down; kill them," but God rose to their defense. He declared, "No, Joshua and Caleb aren't going to die; you're going to die." And a lot of those unbelieving men died immediately.

Joshua and Caleb waited on the Lord. They served faithfully and diligently, looking expectantly toward the day when the people would be ready to reap the harvest. Let me ask you: *Are you ready to reap your harvest?* If so, declare, "I've had enough of not receiving my harvest. I'm ready to go and possess what God has for me." Remember, those who are **willing** and **obedient** will possess what God has promised.

It's Time to Cross Over

Let's read Joshua 1:1–7, "Now after the death of Moses the servant of the Lord it came to pass, that the Lord spake unto Joshua the son of Nun, Moses' minister, saying, Moses my servant is dead; now therefore arise, go over this Jordan, thou, and all this people, unto the land which I do give to them, *even* to the children of Israel. Every place that the sole of your foot shall tread upon, that have I given unto you, as I said unto Moses. From the wilderness and this Lebanon even unto the great river, the river Euphrates, all the land of the Hittites, and unto the great sea toward the going down of the sun, shall be your coast. There shall not any man be able to stand before

Harvest Principle VII: Discern Your Harvest

thee all the days of thy life: as I was with Moses, so I will be with thee: I will not fail thee, nor forsake thee. Be strong and of a good courage: for unto this people shalt thou divide for an inheritance the land, which I sware unto their fathers to give them. Only be thou strong and very courageous, that thou mayest observe to do according to all the law, which Moses my servant commanded thee: turn not from it to the right hand or to the left, that thou mayest prosper whithersoever thou goest."

When I read this, I know that if I don't do what He reveals for me to do, at the time He tells me to do it—when I die, the word of the Lord will be given to someone else to carry out. I'm not going to sleep through my harvest! I'm going to believe God and cross over into the Promised Land.

Notice that God said, "...the land I DO give to them"—not the land that *I'm going to give them*. When God tells you where the harvest is, it's already yours! Remember, a spiritual harvest must come in your heart before it can manifest in the natural realm. God didn't say, "I'm going to give you the land someday." He told Joshua to go into the land that He'd already given them. That's present tense. In other words, if the Lord tells you that a certain car is yours, and then when you get to that car there are no keys and the Sheriff is sitting in front of it, that doesn't make a difference. It's already yours. Why? **God said it.**

This raises another point. When God told Joshua, "...that have I given unto you, as I said unto Moses. From the wilderness and this Lebanon even unto the great river, the river Euphrates, all the land of the Hittites..." This revealed that some *dispossessions* had to take place. Somebody was already in the land...the Hittites. God continued, "...and unto the great sea toward the going down of the sun, shall be your coast. There shall not any man be able to stand before thee..." Right after God told Joshua about the Hittites, He declared that no enemy would be able to stand in his way.

God kept reassuring Joshua, "As I was with Moses, so I will be with thee: I will not fail thee, nor forsake thee." But here's the condition, "Be strong and of a good courage: for unto this people shalt thou divide an inheritance the land, which I sware unto their fathers to give them."

God swore to give the land to Israel's fathers, but the fathers didn't possess it, so He had to pass it on to their children. The fathers slept through their hour of opportunity, so He gave the promise to the children with this condition, "Only be thou strong and very courageous, that thou mayest observe to do according to all the law, which Moses my servant commanded thee: turn not from it to the right hand or to the left, that thou mayest prosper whithersoever thou goest."

When reading these scriptures, does it appear to you that God wants to keep prosperity away from His people? No! Yet remember, there's always an "IF" condition when you're harvesting. God didn't show me that He was moving on my behalf until I learned to consistently say *yes* to His instructions. God will teach you how to harvest, but it's going to start off with instruction in simple areas.

I used to ride the train to work and when I got off the train, I'd walk another few blocks to the office. While walking to the office, God would say, "Turn this way and go down this block," and I'd turn that way and think, *Oh, yeah, I'm going to meet somebody today and this is going to be my day.* Then I'd walk down the block and the only thing that would happen is I'd end up at the office. The next day while walking to work, He'd say, "Go up two blocks, turn around and come down." I'd say, *Okay, this is the day God's going to move.* And He'd move me right to my office. After about a month of God saying, "Go this way," and, "Go that way," I said, "God, why do You keep making me do all these *loop-the-loops* if You're not going to do anything?"

His response was powerful, "I just want you to learn to obey Me whether you're going to get something or not. I want you to learn how to hear My voice, say *yes*, and do what I say when I say to do it. You've been confessing prosperity, but you don't know how to obey My voice. And if you miss your hour of opportunity, don't cry to Me." If this sounds familiar, God is trying to teach you in this season how to be in the right place at the right time, so when the tree falls the fruit will land right outside your doorstep. The problem is, most of us are *over here* when the blessing lands *over there*. So let God begin to deal with the sensitivity of your heart and your level of obedience—because that's the measure that will determine what you sow and reap.

Be honest with yourself. More importantly, be instantly obedient to God's voice. Your heavenly Father is trying to lead you into your land of promise.

Pray and Declare Your Harvest!

Lift your hands to the Lord and pray with me. "Father God, give me ears that can clearly hear Your voice and eyes that can see in the realm of the Spirit so that I can discern the harvest. Help me to perceive and receive it in the Spirit. I will be willing, obedient, and diligent to go exactly where You tell me to go and reap the harvest—whether it may be to the north, south, east, or west. Make me sensitive to the leading of the Holy Spirit. Lord, I willingly offer You everything that I am and everything that You've given me. Use whatever You will from my life for Your glory. I trust You completely, Lord, and I praise You because I know that You are not unjust to forget my labors of love or any seeds that I sow into Your kingdom. I know that Your Word is true and that I will reap in due season if I faint not. I praise You for the one hundredfold return.

"Like Joshua and Caleb, I will not sleep through my harvest. My heart will receive Your wisdom as I watch and pray, and at Your direction I will be ready to go and reap. I am not afraid of any giants; by Your strength and power, I will dispossess them all. I can do all things through Christ as He gives me strength. Right now, Lord, I rededicate myself to You. I give myself to You fully, completely, and without reservation. If there is anything in my past or present that will keep me from crossing over and reaping in my land of promise, show me now, Lord. Create in me a clean heart and renew a right spirit within me…so that I can see as You see, go where You tell me to go, and follow You into my destiny. I thank You and praise You, Father God, in Jesus' name. Amen."

HARVEST PRINCIPLE VII
SEVEN WAYS TO DISCERN YOUR HARVEST

Discern the One Hundredfold Blessing
Mk. 10:17–30, 1 Tim. 6:17 and 12

Discern the Size of Your Harvest
Eccl. 11:1–3, Gen. 25:29–34

Discern If it's Time to Reap
Jn. 4:35, Num. 13:30–33, Ps. 126:1–6

Discern Where the Harvest is Located
Lk. 5:1–7

Discern How Much You Are Able to Reap
Num. 14:5–9, Josh. 1:2 and 6

Discern Your Hour of Opportunity
Prov. 10:4–5, Jn. 3:8, Matt. 26:36–41

Discern Your Level of Obedience to His Voice
Eccl. 11:4, Josh. 1:1–7

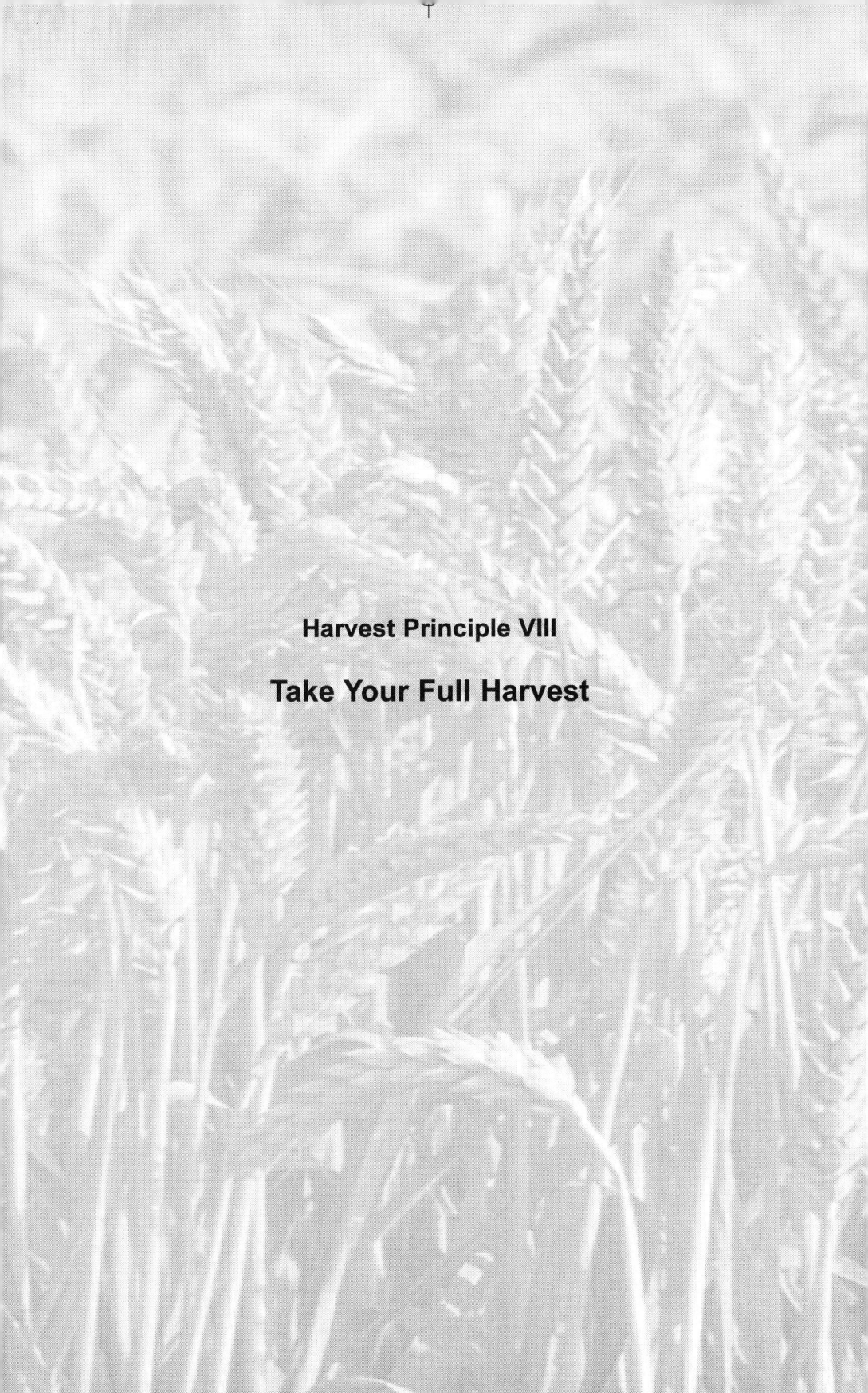

Harvest Principle VIII

Take Your Full Harvest

- 43 -
Declare Victory in the Spirit

Have you ever wondered why so many Christians try to *name it and claim it?* Like I said before, it takes a lot more than just *saying something* to maintain victory in the Spirit. We have to get beyond merely naming and claiming our blessings. Let's look at this on a deeper level.

Many people like to use Mark 11:23–24, "...whosoever shall say unto this mountain, Be thou removed, and be thou cast into the sea; and shall not doubt in his heart, but shall believe those things which he saith shall come to pass; he shall have whatsoever he saith. Therefore I say unto you, what things soever ye desire, when ye pray, believe that ye receive them and ye shall have them."

I had always thought this scripture meant, "When you pray, believe that you have it, and it's yours." In other words, confess it, believe it, and have it. Let's take a closer look at what Jesus was really saying. The Greek meaning for the word, *receive,* is *to take* (Strong's 2983). So we could actually read it this way, "When you pray, believe that you *take* or possess it..."

Now, let's dig a little deeper. We often think that to *possess* means to literally have something in our possession. But remember when God told the Israelites to go and possess the land, He was instructing them to go and *take* charge of it. This word *possession* (as briefly mentioned in the last section) implies an unspoken word...*dispossession.* For example, if you don't pay your rent, management will possess (take) the apartment away from you—but to take possession, they have to first *dispossess* you before they can possess what you currently occupy. The technical term for this is eviction.

In the process of taking (possessing) the harvest that belongs to you, you'll have to do some dispossessing first. This can be very interesting, because God will say, "That's your land. I've given it to you." Then you say, "Glory! Yes! Praise You, Jesus! Hallelujah!" And like Joshua and the second generation of Israelites, when you go to take that land, you'll discover that "others" are already living there holding all of your possessions...and you have to run them off. That's when you start thinking, *God, You didn't tell me about these big, ugly, hairy, musky, stinking demons.* You have to remember, the devil is always doing his job...you simply need to be more proficient at your job than he is at his.

Stand your ground! Rest in the fact that God isn't powerless and the devil isn't in charge. The devil is defeated; he's a punk. The only thing that I ever want to say to the devil is, "Get thee behind me." That's the extent of any conversation I'd have with the enemy because I know who I am in Christ. I'm seated in heavenly places. If the devil has something that belongs to me, he's not going to have it for long. I believe the harvest is already mine; therefore, I know I can take it.

Declare the victory that God has given you and then move forward to possess. That mountain has to move!

- 44 -
Put Your Feet Down...

God gave me a powerful revelation one day. He told me, "People love to say, 'Whatever I put my hands to shall prosper.' " Then He said something that really struck me, "Putting your hands to something isn't a guarantee that you're going to get anything out of it." I'd never heard anything like that before.

You can put your *hands* to someone's ministry or business, but that doesn't mean a part of it will belong to you when it prospers. People who like to put their hands to things aren't taking any responsibility for their ultimate success or failure. Sometimes they just want to be noticed or to ride on someone else's coat tails...all the while thinking: *This ministry's going to take off. I'm going to be seen on television, and when that happens, I'm going to make sure the camera is focused on me.*

Let's look at God's perspective. Joshua 1:3 says, "Every place that the sole of your foot shall tread upon, that have I given unto you..." In other words, when you put your hands to something, it's not necessarily yours; but when you put your *feet* into it, you'll get a different result. Here's an example: Do you simply attend your church, or do you say, "This is my church"? If you were attending our church and I heard you saying, "This is my church...my pastor...our service...our ministry," then I'd know you have your feet in it.

Too many people are looking for something to put their hands to—but if you want to take a harvest, you have to put your feet down. I've noticed that "hands only" Christians say things like, "Pastor, you know what I think we should do? We should start services a little later...I think this...I think that." Here's what I do to "hands only" suggestion people. I tell them to put it in writing and submit it. You'd be amazed at how quickly they'll say, "Oh, I figured I could just tell you." The truth is; they just want to put their hands to something. They're not going to put their feet down and commit to anything. Putting your feet into something requires a serious commitment.

Let's go back to the twelve spies who were instructed to spy out the Promised Land. Ten of them came back and said, "There are giants in the land—we're like grasshoppers—we can't take it." But Joshua and Caleb said, "Yes, we can. Let's not be fools. Let's listen to God and go take it." The majority of the people wanted to kill Joshua and Caleb, but in the end, the uncommitted (unfaithful) Israelites died.

In the face of impossible odds, Joshua and Caleb remained faithful. And remember, this "spy job" wasn't a prominent position. Basically, the spies were expendable. Think about it. They were sent to spy out enemy lands without weapons or any military support (an army, a few troops, or even a few soldiers); so if they had been caught, they would most likely have died. Those twelve spies might not ever have returned to the Israelites' camp.

So how did Joshua end up with his own book in the Bible? How did he become a leader of the Israelites? He went from being a security guard to becoming the head of the nation because he believed God and was willing to DO what God said—despite what everybody else had to say. That's how he became Moses' successor. Being faithful to the leading of God brings great rewards, especially if you're willing to put your feet in whatever He reveals for you to do.

You can put your hands to something and still be ninety-five percent uncommitted—because physically, you can put your hands *over there* and still leave your body *over here*. But you can't put your feet down unless you cross over to the other side…completely.

- 45 -

Don't Lose Heart

Never despise small beginnings. (See Job 8:7, Luke 13:18–19, and Zechariah 4:10.) Joshua and Caleb didn't despise carrying the seed of God's promises to Israel; they put their feet down on the word of the Lord, and then waited forty years before they could go in and possess the new land. Imagine what it was like to sit in the wilderness for forty years waiting for the unbelievers to die off. Nevertheless, through

Harvest Principle VIII: Take Your Full Harvest

faith and patience, Joshua and Caleb waited for their hour of opportunity—and they reaped an awesome harvest.

Again, the fact that they waited on the Lord didn't mean they were sitting back, doing nothing. I believe they waited expectantly on the Lord and remained faithful, and this kept them on track. Joshua was Moses' assistant, so as he was waiting he continued to serve. He didn't become weary in well doing, and he ultimately received an impartation from the Lord through Moses—one that ensured he'd be able to lead the children of Israel to victory. Joshua's season of serving Moses was his divine preparation for leadership.

What about you? You may have great vision and great harvests ahead of you. The Lord may have spoken clearly to you saying, "You're going to do great things." If so, you probably said, "Yes, Lord! I receive it!" At first, joy and excitement were there...but if you started rationalizing what God spoke in your spirit, talking to a few family members, and so on, a different attitude could have surfaced. All too quickly, you could have ended up saying, "Yes, God, whatever You say..." and at the same time have been thinking, *Maybe I'm not supposed to have that anyway.* **If you're not careful, unbelief can creep in.**

This is why you have to keep serving as you wait upon the Lord, because it's all too easy to start out with boldness, and then lose persistence to see the vision through to completion. Let's say God tells you, "You're going to be a multi-millionaire." Initially, you'd be so excited and think, *It's going to happen before this week is over...* So you dive into whatever God tells you to do with both hands and feet. Then when the promise doesn't start unfolding right away, you lose heart and say, "Lord, just let me stick with my sanitation job; just leave me alone."

That's exactly what happened with Moses' generation. God said, "You're going to take the land. *It's yours.* I've given it to you." Then Moses told the spies to go and look at the land and return with a report. They went to Canaan and looked at all of the land. I can imagine one spy saying, "Whoa! That's a lot of land. We don't need all of that...and look at those giants." In response, another says, "Oh, yeah, you need to come over to my side. The giants over here are a lot bigger than the giants you're looking at." "No way!" "Yeah, they're about five times bigger!" Of course, I'm adding drama to this story, but the end result was that the spies decided they couldn't go in and possess what God had already given them.

Later, after crossing over into the Promised Land, Joshua took a different approach. Instead of sending spies to check out the whole land, he targeted one city at a time—and he didn't send twelve spies...he only sent two. I guess that Joshua figured, *Caleb and I came back with the right report, so let's keep the reconnaissance team at two. Two seems to be a good number.* Joshua strategically and wisely seized each divine opportunity.

Have you ever heard the saying, "Inch-by-inch, it's a cinch"? This means as you move forward to possess your harvest, you sometimes have to take the land in small chunks instead of trying to surmount the whole vision at one time. Proceeding too quickly can overwhelm you and make you lose heart. Let's say, for example, that God says you're going to own a certain company. You might have to start by getting a job at that company, maybe even in the mailroom (if that's what God leads you to do).

When accessing new territory, keep your eyes on God, keep serving and don't lose heart. Every step will bring you closer to your harvest.

- 46 -
Be Willing to Share

Have you ever found an item on sale at the grocery store for such a good price that you thought; *I could get five loaves of this bread for the price of one?* Then you bought five loaves, brought them home, and tried to stuff all of them in your refrigerator, thinking, *They're mine.* Before you could eat all of those loaves, they would mold or rot and have to be thrown away.

I've learned that if I go to the store and get several loaves of bread for the price of one, maybe it's because I need to divide it up. If I spread it around, somebody else can be a beneficiary of that blessing. I'm careful not to take more than I can actually use productively at one time, because anybody can take too much of what's set before them. Surplus can look so inviting.

Psalm 139:1–6 exalts God for His sovereignty and also teaches us that we are not to exercise ourselves in things that are "too wonderful" for our understanding. This is why you have to start taking ground one step at a time. If you happen to take more ground than you can handle, bring some other people in. Let them enjoy the blessing with you. Believe me; you'll go a lot further. But if you say, "No, this is mine," then most of the time you'll end up losing it anyway...just like those loaves of bread. If you take too much for you alone to carry, then you're going to drop it. Remember the abundance of fish in Luke 5:1–7. Like those disciples, you must learn to bring others in with you.

Sharing is important to reaping a full harvest. Let's say you plant seeds and then at harvest time you have more than you expected—that's a bumper crop. Your first thought might be, *I'm going to reap this all by myself. I'm not going to hire anybody to help me. This is all mine.* How much are you realistically going to be able to reap? You have to bring somebody in to help you in the reaping process. Don't be stingy. Hire somebody and gather more crops!

God likes to bless "exceedingly abundantly," so if you want to reap wealth correctly, you have to learn how to bring other people in. Remember...*One percent of a hundred people's efforts is better than one hundred percent of your own.* Share your blessings. Spread them around. Give a portion to seven or eight...and if you can't afford to pay the people you bring in, go to somebody and say, "I'll give you a whole acre if you'll help me to harvest the other four acres." If you don't have the capacity to reap five acres, don't let part of a good harvest stay in the field. The key to being blessed is helping other people to receive a blessing. This is the heart of God.

Remember, when you only think of "me and mine," you have stinking thinking. It's like saying, "Well, Pastor, I have to make sure that I get mine first. Then after I get mine, I'm going to help Brother So-and-so...I can't help him right now; but whatever I have left over, don't worry. I'm going to look out for him." Chances are this type of person isn't going very far in the things of God. However, the one who says, "Brother, I'm on my way and I want you to come with me because there's going to be more than I can carry," *that person* has tapped into the heart of God. He or she is a true beneficiary.

Let's pause here and pray. Declare this out loud, "Right now, I bind and renounce every demon of selfishness. Amen." Now say, "I'm not selfish. I'm prosperous in the things of God. I'm a sower. I'm going to share my harvest and spread it around." Now, be still and feel the supernatural release in your spirit!

- 47 -
Help Someone Else to Reap

Have you ever wondered what happened to Caleb? God gave me a simple revelation from the fourteenth chapter of Joshua. We can learn a lot from what Caleb said:

Harvest Time: What's That All About?

> Then the children of Judah came unto Joshua in Gilgal: and Caleb the son of Jephunneh the Kenezite said unto him, Thou knowest the thing that that the Lord said unto Moses the man of God concerning me and thee....Forty years old *was* I when Moses the servant of the Lord sent me from Kadesh-barnea to espy out the land; and I brought him word again as *it was* in mine heart. Nevertheless my brethren that went up with me made the heart of the people melt: but I wholly followed the Lord my God. And Moses sware on that day, saying, Surely the land whereon thy feet have trodden shall be thine inheritance, and thy children's for ever, because thou hast wholly followed the LORD my God. And now, behold, the LORD hath kept me alive, as he said, these forty and five years, even since the LORD spake this word unto Moses, while *the children of* Israel wandered in the wilderness: and now, lo, I *am* this day fourscore and five years old. As yet I *am as* strong this day as I *was* in the day that Moses sent me: as my strength *was* then, even so *is* my strength now, for war, both to go out, and to come in. Now therefore give me this mountain, whereof the LORD spake in that day; for thou heardest in that day how the Anakims were there, and *that* the cities *were* great *and* fenced: if so be the LORD *will be* with me, then I shall be able to drive them out, as the LORD said (vv. 6–12).

Caleb encouraged his friend, Joshua. He reminded Joshua of three things: First, that he had remained true to the Lord even when his brethren didn't; Second, that Moses had confirmed the land would be his inheritance forever because he'd wholly followed the Lord. And third, even though Caleb was old, he was still strong and willing to go with Joshua...no matter what. Get this in your spirit, because this is how you can possess the land and take the harvest God has set aside for you.

Caleb, an eighty-five-year old man, was saying to Joshua, "I'm ready to take the enemy out; I want my land. I've waited for forty years and now I'm ready. I want what's mine." Caleb wasn't afraid. He picked a land that had a fierce army; so in the natural, the odds were definitely against him. Undaunted, he declared the victory, "God was with me then, God is with me now. We've waited forty years, so let's go take this land. I'm ready. It's time for the enemy to give up what is ours." Caleb knew that he'd sown for forty years and it was time to reap. He said, "I want that spot right there with all the beautiful trees, giants, fortresses...everything. I want it all."

Caleb didn't limit how much harvest he could take. He saw himself as being victorious. No one could tell Caleb how much land he was allowed to have—he made that decision on his own.

Harvest Principle VIII: Take Your Full Harvest

Let's examine the other side. It's pretty dangerous to make people, who are believing God for their harvest, lose their faith and zeal. We have to be careful in our "so-called" sharing (i.e., giving people balance) that we don't become responsible for making their hearts melt. If you're going to speak into someone's situation, you'd better make sure that your counsel is from God—because if you're responsible for making that person lose God's vision, you're going to reap that harvest as well. A good rule of thumb is this: If you don't have something good to say (something that's from God), don't say anything at all.

Some time ago, one of the ministers at our church came and told me that God had put it on his heart to become a boxer. At the time, we were both nearly forty years old. While I stood there looking at him, my mind was saying, *Ooh. Wait a minute. You've been afraid to fight all of your life, and now you're going into the ring to let people punch you as a profession? And you're not even going to get paid for this?* My mind continued, *He's not all there. He'll get over this in a couple of days...hopefully. Let me go pray and fast.*

As a leader, the wisdom of God had taught me to be careful not to harm someone else's spirit. So I stepped back and thought, *Well, this isn't sinful...it's not an evil thing. Nobody has to hit me! Let him box. I'll lay hands on his bruises.*

I could have stood there and systematically talked him out of where he perceived that God was leading him—and ended up being responsible for "melting" his heart. If you've ever been guilty of melting a heart or causing someone to lose sight of God's vision, take a moment to repent right now. Then let it go and move forward. Always remember that when you help someone else to reap, it's one of the best ways for you to take your full harvest.

- 48 -

Know It's Never Too Late

From reading about Joshua and Caleb, you should realize that you're never too old to start over or to continue in the things of God. There's no such thing as being "too old" in God's kingdom. So if you're thinking, *I have my pension...I just want to kick back and take it easy,* you can do that if you want to, but remember—Caleb was still going strong at eighty-five years old. He said, "As yet I *am as* strong this day as I *was* in the day that Moses sent me: as my strength *was* then, even so *is* my strength now, for war, both to go out, and to come in" (Joshua 14:11).

That was a pretty bold statement. Remember, the Promised Land was actually Joshua and Caleb's proving ground. At this point, Caleb had proven his strength for five years on the battlefield. Wouldn't you say that made him a doer of the word and not a hearer only? He had waited for years on the other side of the Jordan…and finally, it was time to take the harvest.

Caleb said, "Now therefore give me this mountain, whereof the LORD spake in that day; for thou heardest in that day how the Anakims *were* there, and *that* the cities *were* great *and* fenced: if so be the LORD *will be* with me, then I shall be able to drive them out, as the LORD said" (v. 12). Oh, I really like this guy! Caleb wasn't moved by what he saw. He didn't choose the land where there weren't any enemies. Not once did he say, "I'm kind of old now. I've been fighting for five years. I don't want as much as I used to—I want as few problems as possible. Just give me a small patch of land over there for my kids, my cows, and my dog. Just let me rest."

No! Caleb wanted to give Israel an advantage. Caleb was so sure that God was with him; he knew that he could defeat the most powerful enemies. He said, "*That's* the one I want. I'm taking that one." Caleb waited, served, and got what he asked for.

Let's read further. "And Joshua blessed him, and gave unto Caleb the son of Jephunneh Hebron for an inheritance. Hebron therefore became the inheritance of Caleb the son of Jephunneh the Kenezite unto this day, because that he wholly followed the LORD God of Israel" (vv. 13–14).

Caleb got his harvest. And after doing so, there was no more mention of the great, fierce warriors that he dispossessed. We can take a lesson from Caleb…it's never too late to reap a rich harvest. With God, all things are possible.

- 49 -
Step Out and Find Out

The Word of God says that Caleb wholly followed the Lord. Let's look at this from a different angle. Do you remember the story in the Book of Daniel about the three Hebrew men who were thrown into the fiery furnace? (See Daniel 3.) They basically said three things just before being thrown into the fire. "Not only is our God able, He will deliver us…and even if He chooses not to deliver us, we still trust Him completely" (see 3:16–18). That was also the heart of Caleb.

Religion has taught us to say, "I don't want to be greedy...just a little bit would be enough." But in both stories—the fiery furnace in Babylon and taking ground in the Promised Land—those men of God walked in absolute confidence. Would you go into a fiery furnace or into a land inhabited by giants if you didn't fully trust in God? That's not *name it* and *claim it* stuff. That's full assurance of who God is and who you are *in Him*.

Here's another point. Who chose Hebron as Caleb's inheritance in Joshua 14:12–14? Did God come down in a vision and tell him, "Go take Hebron?" No! Caleb made that choice. Yet, after making the choice he had to be confident enough to step out and do it. This is where a lot of Christians fail to reap. You can't just sit back, thinking, *Hmm, I wonder if God wanted me to have that city?* If so, five years from now, you'd still be sitting there *wondering*.

Step out and find out if God is with you. Remember, you can't steer a parked car. If you're moving, God can turn your wheel one way or the other. Personally, I always want to maintain a confident attitude that's ready to take more of the harvest. Is your confidence rising?

Now, let's look briefly at the flip side. Some preach what I call the "word of suffering," supposedly clothed in humility. In this lying humility doctrine, everything speaks about suffering. I can't put on gospel music without hearing phrases like, "Through the storm...through the cold beating me down, stepping on me...God give me strength for one more day." That's not the gospel! Jesus said the gospel is good news. If the devil's stepping all over you, that's not good news.

Yes, there are troubles in this world. I would never try to tell you otherwise. The world today is filled with terrorism, anxieties, and a multitude of sins (see Romans 1:29–31). However, Jesus told us not to worry, "...In the world ye shall have tribulation: but be of good cheer; I have overcome the world" (see John 16:29–33). Meditate on this...let it really sink into your spirit.

I'm like Caleb. If the enemy raises his head; I'm taking it off.

- 50 -

Never Compromise with the Enemy

Now that we've covered the kind of attitude that takes more of the harvest, let's go to Joshua 17 and look at the attitude that doesn't. Caleb had a persistent heart, but let's see what happened with everybody else. These were the so-called humble people, because they learned how to disguise their lack of initiative with humility. In reality, they were lazy and did not have any backbone. Let's see what the Word has to say:

Harvest Time: What's That All About?

> And Manasseh had in Issachar and in Asher Bethshean and her towns, and Ibleam and her towns, and the inhabitants of Dor and her towns, and the inhabitants of Endor and her towns, and the inhabitants of Taanach and her towns, and the inhabitants of Megiddo and her towns, *even* three countries. Yet the children of Manasseh could not drive out *the inhabitants of* those cities; but the Canaanites would dwell in that land. Yet it came to pass, when the children of Israel were waxen strong, that they put the Canaanites to tribute; **but did not utterly drive them out.** And the children of Joseph spake unto Joshua, saying, Why hast thou given me *but* one lot and one portion to inherit, seeing *I am* a great people, forasmuch as the Lord hath blessed me hitherto?
>
> And Joshua answered them, If thou *be* a great people, *then* get thee up to the wood *country*, and cut down for thyself there in the land of the Perizzites and of the giants, if mount Ephraim be too narrow for thee. And the children of Joseph said, The hill is not enough for us: and all the Canaanites that dwell in the land of the valley have chariots of iron, *both they* who *are* of Bethshean and her towns, and *they* who *are* of the valley of Jezreel.
>
> And Joshua spake unto the house of Joseph, *even* to Ephraim and to Manasseh, saying, Thou *art* a great people, and hast great power: thou shalt not have one lot *only*: But the mountain shall be thine; for it *is* a wood, and thou shalt cut it down: and the outgoings of it shall be thine: for thou shalt drive out the Canaanites, though they have iron chariots, *and* though they be strong (Joshua 17:11–18).

Here's the bottom line: The children of Manasseh couldn't drive out the enemy. They'd prayed and worked on this issue long enough, so they finally decided. "Well, we can't get them out so we'll just let them live with us. We'll make them work for us—but we won't run them out." That was a treaty with the devil. It was like saying, "I've been praying about this cancer…arthritis…asthma for a couple of years and nothing has happened, so I'll just leave it alone. I'm blessed in other ways." Are you getting this? How could you be satisfied in God while you're living with something He died and rose again to deliver you from?

Saved people will go around declaring, "I've got faith, baby. I bind devils and cast out demons…do you need me to pray for you? In the name of Jesus…" and so on. Then they turn around and go to the leader, saying, "Why did you give us this little bit of land? We've got all these people and we need more stuff." Why did the Manassites need Joshua's help? Instead of taking their own land, they put the pressure on their leader...and he didn't take the bait. Joshua told them, "Go take them out."

What a contrast. Just a few chapters earlier, an eighty-five-year-old man (Caleb) said, "Give me the most fortified city," and he took it. Then these young boys came up to Joshua, talking about how great, mighty, and full of faith they were—expecting Joshua to take the land for them. They cried, "Giants are over there. They've got chariots, iron, and other things!"

The tribe of Manasseh created its own problem. They had already made a treaty with the enemy so they were living in the same space. Manasseh was in a Catch 22 situation—so they were already in a losing battle. Then they tried to go to the man of God and make him feel like he'd done some injustice. Pay close attention. These people created their own problem because they didn't have "uncompromising" hearts.

Don't make treaties. Don't punk out. If you have to stop and catch your breath during the battle, then stop and do so—but don't give any ground to the enemy, because when it's time to drive out the enemy, you'll be exposed. Never compromise your position of authority. You'll only have to gain it back later.

- 51 -
Rise to Greatness in God

Remember, how much of the harvest you're going to take depends on you. Don't sit idly by wishing God would bless you like He's blessing somebody else. Maybe that person took some painful steps that you don't know about. He or she could have believed God against hope in situations that looked like they would never end...but in the eternal view, they only lasted a moment.

You have to be willing to step out. When we stepped out and got our own office, we didn't have any money, and I took a lot of persecution. Then when I started to make some money, people were still persecuting me. "Well, why do you want to get an office downtown? You don't need to pay that kind of rent..." Blah, blah, blah.

One day, a friend of mine was saying, "You have a family. You can't make these kinds of moves..." I turned it back on him, "Let me tell you something," I said. "You've been working for the same company for seventeen years and are looking forward to receiving a pension. When you retire, that's all you'll have to talk about. But I'll be able to say that I owned my own business, did some traveling, and took some chances. Some succeeded and some failed, but nonetheless, I stepped out. What are you going to say? 'Yeah, I was faithful to contribute to social security for seventy-five years and now I get my check every week'?"

Understand something. Great men and women take chances. Don't let anything hinder you; when God speaks, step out. Rise to greatness. Think about great men in the Bible. Did God say, "Leave where you are and go to that exact place over there?" Remember, God told Abram to go to a land he didn't know, had never seen, and knew nothing about (see Genesis 12:1).

If God is speaking to your heart right now, just be honest and say, "Lord, I can see that I've missed some opportunities. You moved and opened doors for me, and I was really excited. I knew it was You, but I let people talk me out of it, or I even talked myself out of it."

There are many dreamers in the world (me included). In fact, many people have said this to me...and I used to feel bad when they said it; but then I woke up to something. Dreamers have important roles to play. If it weren't for dreamers, the non-dreamers wouldn't have employment. If you're a dreamer, this should be charging you up!

When the Manassites came to Joshua whining and saying, "You didn't give us enough land," they were approaching God's representative—so in a sense they were coming to God saying, "You didn't give me enough." To put this in street language, Joshua "flipped the script and put it back on them." He said, "Get yourself up and go get your own land." Joshua didn't carry them.

I'm not a "carry-you" Pastor. That's why we're called Joshua and Caleb Ministries. I'd tell you in a minute, "There's the land, get in there, cut down some trees, and make yourself some space. There's no carrying here." Helping, yes. Carrying, no. We help as God says to help, because when you're learning, you're learning...but ultimately, a point will come when someone comes to me and says, "I'm a great faith person." I'll say, "Alright"...and if he or she comes back to me whining about something, I'll say, "Get yourself up. Get on into the land, because you are great." Joshua was encouraging the Manassites when he said they could drive out the enemies. It was all a matter of perception.

Harvest Principle VIII: Take Your Full Harvest

Now, lets go to Joshua chapter eighteen and see what happened to the remaining tribes of Israel, "And the whole congregation of the children of Israel assembled together at Shiloh, and set up the tabernacle of the congregation there. And the land was subdued before them. And there remained among the children of Israel seven tribes, which had not yet received their inheritance" (vv. 1–2).

Seven of the twelve tribes didn't receive their land. That means more than sixty percent of the nation of Israel didn't get what rightfully belonged to them. They were going in, witnessing miracles and victories, seeing old man Caleb go take his land…but more than fifty percent of the tribes still hadn't reaped any part of their own harvest. Does that sound like the body of Christ today? More than fifty percent still don't have their land. Sadly, this isn't a new thing. It's relatively common.

Let's continue reading in verse three, "And Joshua said unto the children of Israel, How long *are* ye slack to go to possess the land, which the Lord God of your fathers hath given you?" In other words, he was telling them it could be done, but they'd have to do it. Nobody was holding them back—they were holding themselves back from taking their full harvest.

Stop right now and say, "I have to do it." Say it like you mean it! Because here's the truth: Others can motivate you…but only you can rise.

- 52 -

Distribute the Surplus

Let's go to Joshua 19:9, "Out of the portion of the children of Judah *was* the inheritance of the children of Simeon: for the part of the children of Judah was too much for them: therefore the children of Simeon had their inheritance within the inheritance of them."

Judah took too much land! Did God rebuke them for that? Do you see anywhere in that verse that God had any complaints? Now, here's the picture. Remember the complainers who were saying, "Why don't we have enough land? We need something else." They were crying because they didn't have enough of what they wanted. On the other hand, Judah (the tribe that Jesus ultimately came from) took too much. Jesus, our Messiah, is the Lion of the tribe of Judah—so there's a definite connection to victory.

Let me summarize how events played out in the earlier books of Joshua. Judah went out, beat the enemy, took a portion of land, and then sent a messenger back to Joshua…"We've possessed the land,

Harvest Time: What's That All About?

now what should we do?" Joshua replied, "Is there any land behind you? If so, go and take it." And that's what they did—then they sent a messenger saying, "We took this land as well." Joshua asked, "What is in front of you? Possess that land." So they took it. After they were finished reaping, it dawned on them, *Oh, my God. There's more land than we can use!*

Then Judah remembered that the tribe of Simeon didn't have enough land, so they gave them part of their inheritance. Judah had reaped such a mighty harvest that when Simeon inhabited their portion of the surplus land, these two tribes still didn't rub elbows. In fact, they couldn't even see each other.

This is the heart it takes to reap, baby. This is the way you get your "pie in the sky" in the land of "milk and honey" while you're here on earth. Reap boldly and divide the spoil! You can wait until you die if you want to, but the provision is here RIGHT NOW. How much of the harvest are you going to take? Remember, if you reap too much God isn't going to be upset with you—just share it with somebody else. Spread it around. The decision is yours.

- 53 -

It's Yours for the Taking

The story of the prodigal son in Luke 15:11–32 relates strongly to where the body of Christ is today concerning the harvest. Let's review. Basically, a wealthy businessman had two sons. The younger son went to his father and asked for his inheritance saying, "I want my part now."

People usually read this and think, *He's got a lot of nerve.* Yet, the father didn't seem to have a problem with his request. (Remember, the father in this story is representative of God and the two boys are representative of God's people.) So the fact that the son asked for his inheritance wasn't the problem. It's what he did with it that was terrible. The scripture tells us that the father gave it to him as he requested. As a result, big brother got his cut because little brother had enough heart to step up and take what was his. In short, big brother benefited from little brother's confidence. (See verse 12.)

Again, many believers today are saying, "I don't want to ask God for too much." At the same time, God is saying, "I'm trying to get you to realize that you're the King's kids. Step out and take what I have already provided for you." But we still want to say, "I don't know, God, I want to be humble."

Harvest Principle VIII: Take Your Full Harvest

Think about it. The only thing that messed little brother up was his motive. Prosperity ruins a fool, because when you get outside of God's will, even if you have a lot of money in your pocket, you're going to go down...there's no way around it.

People talk badly about little brother, but I like the fact that he humbled himself and returned to his father. In fact, I like little brother better than big brother. When I finish this story, you'll understand why. On the way home, little brother was rehearsing, *Hmm, I've got to get back in the house. How am I going to do that now? I know I've messed up all the money dad gave me and I know dad has to be upset; but I don't care. I can't keep living like this...Aha! I know what I'm going to do.* I'm going to go home and say, "Dad, let me be a slave. Let me work for you. I'll just take a little job. Pay me a minimum wage."

Little brother didn't care what he had to do...he just wanted to get back in his father's house. I can hear him thinking, *I'm going to be a son again in a couple of miles. I'm going to get back in there any way that I can.* Little brother was ready to repent and work things out. And when he had come close enough for his father to see him, he discovered that his father was filled with compassion. He ran to little brother, hugged him, kissed him, gave him the finest clothing, and then held a big celebration in his honor.

Seeing all of this, big brother was beside himself—he was really mad. He fumed, "I'm not going to his party. I don't care. I'm going to stay right out here. They can laugh and dance all they want." Then big brother sat outside on the porch so that he could hear everything that was happening at the party. He soaked it all in. Everybody was laughing and having fun, and he was sitting outside sulking. Being offended will rob you of your blessings every time. Big brother was outside, so he was missing the blessings.

The father came out to him and said, "What's your problem? Why are you sitting out here? Why aren't you in the party?" Big brother said, "I don't want to join the party, because I've been here with you...I've been faithful. I've been by your side; I've never left you. *He ran off and wasted all of his money (your money)*—yet you're throwing a party for him. You've never thrown a party for me." The father responded, "Now, wait a minute. You have never left me, and everything I have is yours. We should be happy because your brother has been restored." You see, if big brother wanted a party, he could have had one anytime. Everything already belonged to him.

God is saying to us today, "Everything I have is yours," not, "I'm going to give you everything someday." Sadly, the body of Christ is a lot like big brother. We say, "I'm serving God, I go to church, I pay my tithe, but I never have anything. And look at *him*. He comes to church once every three months and God blessed *him* with a new car." Maybe he simply had enough faith to step up and say, "Dad, I want to take that land over there and if You'll be with me, I'm going to take it." All of his life, big brother had been humble. He stayed at home, did the right things, yet he ended up feeling like he was doing without. False humility is empty.

The father had already given both of his sons the inheritance (see Luke 15:12). Big brother didn't believe it was his to spend and little brother did. Big brother was crying because he didn't get a party, when in fact, he'd received just as much money as little brother had received. So in a capsule…big brother is like believers who are in the kingdom, loving and serving God, yet doing without. Does this sound familiar? If this sounds like your experience with God, then it's definitely time to change.

- 54 -
Walk in Your God-given Authority

It's important that you know the Lord's promises are yours today. Just walk up to that heavenly boardroom, knock on the door and say, "Dad, I need to see you a minute. I know you're in a board meeting, but this is important. I need to talk to you…I've come for my inheritance and I want to know what I need to do." Then the Father will say, "I'll tell you what to do. Look around. Find some land, plot it out, go after it, and I'll back it up."

Remember what Jesus said to the disciples in Luke 10:18–20, "And He said to them, I saw Satan falling like a lightning [flash] from heaven. Behold! I have given you authority {and} power to trample upon serpents and scorpions, and [physical and mental strength and ability] over all the power that the enemy [possesses]; and nothing shall in any way harm you. Nevertheless, do not rejoice at this, that the spirits are subject to you, but rejoice that your names are enrolled in heaven" (Ampl.). In other words, know who you are in Christ and do whatever He tells you to do—because you can rejoice that you are a son or daughter in His eternal kingdom. You have already been given power and authority over the enemy.

Harvest Principle VIII: Take Your Full Harvest

So, look around. Survey the land. See what bears witness in your heart, and then start reaping.

When God began to prosper me financially, it humbled me tremendously. Even now, when I see what God is doing in light of what He's already done, I realize just how big He really is…and weep.

When it was time for me to reap my harvest, I didn't just sit at home singing, "Kumbaya." I had to step out. I had to let go of some things that I had been trusting in—and that put me in the posture to trust God. You can do the same. When you do, a rich harvest will be inevitable.

Harvest Time: What's That All About?

Harvest Principle VIII: Take Your Full Harvest

Pray and Declare Your Harvest!

Let's pray…"Father God, we give You the praise and thank You for the power of Your Word. Thank You for the truth and integrity of Your Word. We thank You that Your Word will never return to You void, but it will accomplish Your purpose. Father, we believe right now, this day, that we are a people wholly justified by You. We don't desire wealth so that we can be wealthy; we desire to be prosperous so that we can be a blessing.

"Lord, we desire to be spiritual storehouses for You, blessing Your kingdom and Your people. Father, we want to be there with the answers that people need. We desire to be like the man in Mark 14:13 who had a pitcher of water and led the disciples to the upper room where they would share their last Passover meal with Jesus. We desire to be like the man in Matthew 21:7 that gave the donkey to the disciples for Jesus' triumphant entry into Jerusalem. We desire to set up a banquet table for You, Lord. We desire to be Your people. Your Word says that You prepare a table for us in the presence of our enemies. We know that we don't have enemies in heaven, so that means a table will be prepared for us here and now.

"Father, we partake of Your table *right now* and believe *right now* that, in the name of Jesus, You'll humble us with Your goodness—for it is Your kindness that leads us to repentance. The blessings of the Lord make us truly rich and You add no sorrow to them. Father, we thank You in the name of Jesus that Your Word says, You know the plans that You have for us…plans to prosper us and not to hurt us, to bring us to an expected end.

"We honor You for this, Lord. We praise You for it. In Jesus' holiest of names, Amen."

HARVEST PRINCIPLE VIII
TWELVE WAYS TO TAKE YOUR FULL HARVEST

Declare Victory in the Spirit
Mk. 11:23–24

Put Your Feet Down Firmly in the Land
Josh. 1:3

Don't Lose Heart
Josh. 1:6, Job 8:7, Lk. 13:18–19, Zech. 4:10

Be Willing to Share Your Harvest with Others
Lk. 5:7, Eccl. 11:1–2

Help Someone Else to Reap
Josh. 14:6–12

Know that It's Never Too Late to Reap a Rich Harvest
Josh. 14:11–14

Step Out and Find Out
Dan. 3:16–18, Josh. 14:12–14, Jn. 16:33

Never Compromise with the Enemy
Josh. 17:11–18

Rise to Greatness in God
Gen. 12:1, Josh. 18:1–4

Distribute the Surplus
Josh. 19:9

Be Settled in the Fact that the Harvest Is Yours
Lk. 15:11–32

Walk in Your God-given Authority!
Lk. 10:18–20

Harvest Principle IX

Sustain Your Land

- 55 -
How Much Ground Are You Going to Keep?

The enemy can never bind the Word of God because God will never be subject to the devil. In light of this, let me ask—How much ground are you going to keep? God's promises aren't limited to one season of reaping.

In 2 Timothy 2:8–10, the apostle Paul said, "Remember that Jesus Christ of the seed of David was raised from the dead according to my gospel [according to the good news, because the gospel is good news]: Wherein I suffer trouble, as an evil doer, *even* unto bonds; but the word of God is not bound. Therefore I endure all things for the elect's sakes, that they may also obtain the salvation which is in Christ Jesus with eternal glory" (emphasis added).

Paul had been whipped, thrown in jail, and endured all types of terrible circumstances, yet he still said, "...the word of God is not bound." The devil can try to get you all bound up, but he can't tie up the Word because it will never return to God void of fulfilling His purpose (see Isaiah 55:10–11). The Word of God always accomplishes the purposes of God. The question is: Will we continue to stand once God has given us the land and we have reaped a mighty harvest? Paul did. He stood his ground.

Salvation doesn't only involve going to heaven when you die. It has an eternal glory. This means when you've received deliverance from the Lord, you shouldn't find yourself back in the same position six weeks (or even six months) later needing deliverance in that same area. Be honest with yourself. Have you ever received a breakthrough and then landed back in bondage again a short time afterwards? Have you ever had a financial need, believed God for deliverance—and then after God brought you out, you landed back in the same financial jam?

Remember the words of Paul, who obeyed the word of the Lord and stood his ground. Think about the spiritual harvest that he reaped! Do you think that Paul gave up any of his harvest, or gave back any of the "land" that God blessed him to take? Absolutely not! Paul's ministry literally changed the world. Whatever he sowed multiplied.

Once you reap your harvest, you need to stand your ground according to Ephesians 6:13, "Wherefore take unto you the whole armour of God, that ye may be able to withstand in the evil day, and having done all, to stand." Read about the rest of your spiritual armor in verses 14–18...because when God gives you an inheritance, He expects you to "occupy" until He comes. Losing ground isn't an option.

- 56 -
Let the Soil Rest

After you have reaped the harvest, it's time for the soil to rest. This takes me back to 2 Timothy 2:10 and the "eternal glory" of our salvation. Your deliverance from God is sure, fixed, real, and permanent. (See John 19:30.) There is no temporary deliverance in the Lord. However, I've had people tell me things like, "Pastor, I really felt that God delivered me, and then I was right back to chasing women again." In this scenario, one of two things happened. First, they mustered up enough willpower to sustain themselves for a while...and when the fleshly desire came back, they went right back to doing what the flesh had become accustomed to doing. Second, they sought God, got a victory, and then concluded that they no longer needed to continue seeking Him. This is why we must learn how to rest in God—how to keep the ground He's given us.

Some of the most committed believers, after experiencing great spiritual victories, have ended up compromising their position. "Oh, God, I'm such a failure," they say, "You taught me to watch my mouth and I haven't cussed for a long time; but this person got me mad and it all just came back out again. I thought I was free, God."

This reveals an important truth: When you've finished reaping the harvest, your focus must turn again to the soil. Remember the principle of plowing? This principle is very similar. Jesus said that when a demon is cast out of a man it wanders around in "dry places." When it can't find a place to rest, it comes back to find its old "home" all cleaned up—so it gets seven more demons to keep it company. And the last state of that man is worse than the first (see Matthew 12:45). This leads to a question...if a demon has been cast out, what would give it permission to move in again and bring seven of its buddies? That man's deliverance wasn't based on eternal salvation in Christ! Eternal glory didn't have any part of it, or the demons wouldn't have been able to gain entry.

True deliverance (from the things that oppress and offend) comes as you continue growing in the things of God. I have gained an understanding of this truth personally, because there were times that God delivered my family out of poverty into a good place and then we found ourselves back in poverty. That's how I know people tend to get comfortable and complacent when their situation starts to improve—and this is the season when they need to be most watchful—because that's when the enemy springs the trap.

By and large, when Christians experience victory we tend to throw our feet up on a stool, lay our heads back and think, *Okay, that's that.* Then the devil starts creeping back in. Hear a word of wisdom from the Lord: If you've gained ground and yet you're not consistently taking ground from the devil, then he's inching in to take ground from you. Simply put, if you're not taking ground, you're losing it.

Be at rest in God and you'll be a real threat to the devil...because as you remain submitted to God and continue to resist the enemy, he has to keep running! *Let the ground rest.* When you reap that mighty harvest, go back to the soil and inspect it. In other words, keep examining your heart and make sure you're in right standing with God. Keep standing on those scriptures that God gave to you before; don't get comfortable and forget where you found them in the Bible. If you do, the very thing you were able to cast down in order to reap will climb back in the ring to duke it out with you again.

- 57 -

Lift Up Your Eyes

When you get into the land of plenty, it's easy to forget the Lord. Deuteronomy 8:11 says, "Beware that thou forget not the LORD thy God, in not keeping his commandments, and his judgments, and his statutes, which I command thee this day..." It's easy to be spiritual when you're experiencing lack, because you have to depend on the Lord just to survive—but when you have reaped a rich harvest it can be easy to forget the many great things God has done in your life. Remember the rich young ruler. He'd done everything right, but because he was afraid to lose his great possessions he still couldn't trust in God.

In whatever state you're in be mindful to not forget the commandments of God, because you'll ultimately get to a place where you no longer keep them. You'll say, "Oh, I know the Word. I remember the Word...oh, yes." That's not the issue. God wants you to maintain your spiritual priorities, and here they are: Number one, don't forget His Word. Number two, don't get so comfortable with God that you're no longer obedient to His voice.

Harvest Principle IX: Sustain Your Land

Remember, the little foxes spoil the vines. Let's say that you rented a movie at Blockbuster and then never returned it...without any intention to pay the late fees or to purchase the video. Then when you read, "Thou shall not steal" (Exodus 20:15), you'd rationalize, *This really isn't stealing, because Blockbuster has insurance anyway. If I don't return this tape, they're not really losing anything. They have guidelines in place to cover it.*

If you were to do this, wouldn't you be forgetting the commandments? Wouldn't you be making the Word of God of no effect? You might remember the Word, but somehow you've created sub-laws to get around doing what's right and true in God's eyes—because you've forgotten Him. Then you'd end up wondering why you had to start boxing with the devil again. You opened the door!

Here's another scenario. God tells you to forgive somebody: a family member, brother or sister in the Lord, or maybe a friend who has wronged you. If you say, "Well, I'll forgive him or her, but I'm never going to forget," then you're a liar—because if you're not going to forget what offended you, then you haven't really forgiven. You can't constantly hold people's sins up before them in judgment. How would you like for God to tell you, "I'm going to forgive you, but I'm never going to forget what you did"?

You can't move forward in any kind of relationship if you won't release the person from what they did to offend you. You also can't expect to keep your blessings. Unforgiveness is one of the quickest "blessing stealers" that I know.

Let's keep reading in Deuteronomy 8, "Lest *when* thou hast eaten and art full, and hast built goodly houses, and dwelt *therein*; and *when* thy herds and thy flocks multiply, and thy silver and thy gold is multiplied, and all that thou hast is multiplied; then thine heart be lifted up, and thou forget the LORD thy God..." (vv. 12–14).

Everybody says, "No way, if God blessed me, I would never forget what He did." Oh, yes, we can—and most of the time, we do. Remember, people tend to think about God most during times of trouble...when we're needy. In times of blessing, however, our hearts can be "lifted up." Most people forget the Lord when things are going well.

I still remember when my family was able to purchase our jeep with cash. Wow! Then a few years ago, we moved into our new home. I just keep thinking and talking about all of the great things that God has done in our lives, because it keeps me in remembrance of Him. Psalm 103:2 says, "Bless the LORD, O my soul, and forget not all his benefits…" Declaring all that God has done for you keeps your heart inclined to His Word instead of becoming focused on what you lack when times are difficult. How much better is it, then, to keep praising Him once you've reached the land of plenty?

When you get blessed and reap a rich harvest to the extent that you don't have to pray about paying rent or bills, don't let your heart be lifted up. Don't lose sight of God. And if your blessing comes through someone else, **guard your heart against elevating that person to the level of God in your life.** Always keep God first and you'll be able to sustain the good land that He's given you.

- 58 -
Keep Your Head Covered

Sustaining your harvest is a serious matter, almost as vital as breaking ground and establishing a strong foundation. In reality, pouring a foundation and laying a roof are the most tedious parts of the building process. Once you lay a foundation, the wood, sheetrock and brick seem to go up in no time. Then once you get to the roof, more attention to detail is necessary. You can break ground, build a beautiful house, and then lose it to the elements because your roof is unstable.

Let's continue with the word of the Lord in Deuteronomy 8:13–16, "…and *when* thy herds and thy flocks multiply, and thy silver and thy gold is multiplied, and all that thou hast is multiplied; then thine heart be lifted up, and thou forget the LORD thy God, which brought thee forth out of the land of Egypt, from the house of bondage, who led thee through that great and terrible wilderness, *wherein were* fiery serpents, and scorpions, and drought, where *there was* no water; who brought thee forth water out of the rock of flint; who fed thee in the wilderness with manna, which thy fathers knew not, that he might humble thee, and that he might prove thee, to do thee good at thy latter end…"

Notice that God didn't prove Himself to Israel by sending serpents; sin brought the suffering. God brought the relief. He proved Himself by covering them. Serpents, scorpions, a water shortage, and people dying didn't come from God. Romans 6:23 tells us that the wages of sin is death. When Israel began to worship idols, they turned their backs on God and walked away from Him. Then sin brought death…but God brought blessing. Why did He bless them?

The scripture tells us that in blessing Israel, God humbled them. The goodness of God leads to repentance. Remember this the next time somebody tells you that some catastrophe in your life took place because God was trying to humble you. That's simply not true! God fed and blessed Israel—that's how He shows His greatness. Think about it. I don't beat up on my kids in order to humble them. I teach them what is right.

In the same way, God will bless you to show you that He's bigger than anything you could ever imagine. Didn't Jesus tell us to bless those who curse us, pray for those who spitefully use us, and to feed our enemies? Why would He tell us to do one thing and then do the opposite Himself? God doesn't desire to kill His children. When people fell by the sword in the Bible, they had either turned their backs on God or come against His people. Sin brought death.

God has put solid ground under our feet and a strong covering over our heads—but we have to learn how to stay inside of the house. We have to stay under His mighty hand…learn to remain humble before Him. When we choose to either follow or disobey God, it's a conscious decision. So remember, even in plenty, stay humble and you'll be blessed in the end. Don't let your heart get lifted up and cause you to lose your blessing. Knowing this truth will definitely make you free from the devil's devices.

Now, let's go back to verses 17 and 18 of the eighth chapter of Deuteronomy: "…and thou say in thine heart, My power and the might of *mine* hand hath gotten me this wealth. But thou shalt remember the LORD thy God: for it is he that giveth thee power to get wealth, that he may establish his covenant which he sware unto thy fathers, as *it is this day.*"

God was saying, "After I've fed you, taken care of you and blessed you; don't start telling everyone that your own intelligence, wisdom, and connections brought you into blessing." In other words, don't act self-righteous. You've probably done this without realizing it, "Oh, yeah, I called Joe and he took care of it for me." This says whatever you received was the result of *your* ideas; *you* made it happen. What would have happened if Joe's number had been changed, or if he didn't have the means to help you? You must recognize that God is your source. He lines up every blessing and does what only He can do so that you can reap a mighty harvest.

God hates a haughty spirit. So stay covered. Humble yourself under His mighty hand.

- 59 -
Be Instant...in Every Season

Jesus is the same yesterday, today and forever (Hebrews 13:8). In other words, He's faithful. If you want to keep your blessings, stay saved and delivered...in other words, *be faithful* to God. Paul urged Timothy, "...Keep your sense of urgency [stand by, be at hand and ready], whether the opportunity seems to be favorable or unfavorable..." (2 Timothy 4:2, Ampl.). Be instant in every season...like that tree in Psalm 1 that's planted by the rivers of water.

It's one thing to obtain a blessing, yet another thing to maintain it. You see, a lot of believers are trying to take their "old junk" and fix it while God keeps saying, "No! You've been born again; old things have passed away...all things have become new." That's why new construction is better than reconstruction. It's nice to buy somebody's old house and fix it up, but it's even better to build a brand new house that's customized just for you. I hear people say all the time that if you buy a used car; you're buying somebody else's problem. Spiritually speaking, the devil constantly tries to force you back into this mold.

Remember, the enemy's ultimate goal isn't to rob your blessings, health, and money. He wants to steal the Word that's in your spirit. Think about the parable of the sower in Matthew 13:18–23. Jesus said the wicked one (the bird) came and immediately took the seeds that had fallen by the wayside (v. 19). Do you see what posture you have to be in for the devil to steal from you? You have to be off track. The devil doesn't care about your possessions. He knows that if he can steal the Word from you, anything you possess will automatically follow.

Whenever I minister about prosperity, people naturally start thinking about money and possessions. You should be convinced now more than ever that "things" are not the proof God has blessed you! Being in the will of God proves that you are truly blessed. Jesus said, "And you, do not seek [by meditating and reasoning to inquire into] what you are to eat and what you are to drink; nor be of anxious (troubled) mind [unsettled, excited, worried, and in suspense]....Only aim at *and* strive for *and* seek His kingdom, and all these things shall be supplied to you also" (Luke 12:29, 31, Ampl.). Be in the will of God and everything else will follow.

Abraham was a man of faith and God prospered him because he was faithful. You see, Abraham didn't seek after what God could do

Harvest Principle IX: Sustain Your Land

for him materially; he was faithful to follow the One who had called him out into a new land. We must understand faithfulness in two ways. First, we are filled with faith from God. Second, we must be faithful to God. In other words, God is able to count on you as you count on Him. It's a covenant relationship. Too often, this principle is missing from faith messages.

Faith encompasses a lot more than just believing God for what you want. Otherwise, God is nothing more than a spiritual genie. People who put God in this category simply find the right scriptures to get what they want and start confessing them. Listen carefully. God isn't obligated to give you goodies. He loves you, but He's not required to give you everything that you "confess." Faith and faithfulness work together. If you truly have faith in God, you'll be committed to what He's entrusted to you…like faithful Abraham.

Think about it. If you can say, "God is faithful, He will do everything that He says He'll do," then why shouldn't God be able to say the same thing about you? The scripture promises us that when we faithfully put His kingdom first, *all these things* (the things that we have need of) will be added—even after we've come through a season of reaping a great harvest! Every day, I'm getting closer to the place where God can say, "If I tell my son to do something, it's going to get done."

Remember what Paul said in 2 Timothy 2:10, "Therefore I endure all things for the elect's sakes…" Who are the elect? The body of Christ. Paul remained faithful so that others could be brought into the kingdom to receive God's manifold blessings. This is true kingdom living. So be "instant." Keep your sense of urgency about the things of God…even after you've reaped a mighty harvest.

- 60 -
Keep Reaching Out

Being unselfish is another great way to maintain your harvest. Proverbs 11:25 says, "The liberal soul shall be made fat: and he that watereth shall be watered also himself." Remember the *little foxes* that spoil the vines…this means the devil is roaming around looking for any open door to invade your blessings. One of the biggest areas of deception is selfishness. Why? King David said, "Who can understand *his* errors? Cleanse thou me from secret *faults*" (Psalm 19:12). Some *little* areas stay hidden…and these areas can jeopardize your entire harvest.

Let me put this in simple terms. You can't always pray for yourself and expect God to bless *only you*. That's selfish. If you can't see past your "field," something's wrong. I've learned that when I'm praying for someone else's need, I can't focus on my own needs; therefore, my problem ceases to be a problem. I've actually received more blessings from God by praying for someone else to be blessed.

This takes me back to Luke 6:30–38, "Give to every man that asketh of thee; and of him that taketh away thy goods ask *them* not again. And as ye would that men should do to you, do ye also to them likewise....Give, and it shall be given to you; good measure, pressed down, and shaken together, and running over, shall men give into your bosom..." Like I said before, we like to use this scripture for finances, but it really covers every area of our lives. If you give love, then love will be given back to you. If you give caring, then you'll reap the same. If you pray for people, **God will raise up others to pray for you.**

Here's how people with a *bless me, gimme* attitude lose their harvest. When God blesses them, their focus comes off of God and onto the things that He's given them. I've actually seen this play out. People say, "Praise God! The Pastor laid hands on me and I got this job..." Afterwards, that was it. The job becomes "God, Jr." They begin to focus everything on keeping that job. Then the boss who liked them so much rises up against them and starts treating them badly. Other people in the office follow suit. Why? The anointing that got the job is gone. They are on their own.

Now, let me clarify. God doesn't leave us; we close our connection with Him by saying, "Genie, get back in the bottle. I'll pour you out when I need you next time...I'll just rub the lamp. For now, get back in there." All too easily, we get caught up in our success and start doing things our way...until the threats return. That's when people run to their pastors saying, "Oh, they're treating me badly, Pastor." Listen to me. Sometimes we need a wake up call to get our focus back on worshipping the Creator and not the creation; the "Bless-er" and not the "bless-ee."

If the devil can get you to trust in that paycheck, he's got you. He'll do everything that he can to oppose you and make you feel insecure. For example, out of nowhere the boss announces, "You can't have overtime. Your hours are being cut." Issues like that always come up when the "thing" that you believed for becomes your source of supply. Watch out! Selfishness is a trap.

Here's another example. Sometimes when you're really believing God to move and you have fewer resources, you tend to give more.

Then when you get blessed with more, you give less. I know that I've been guilty of this. I was believing God to move when I didn't have much money, so I sowed seed every chance I got. Then when the money started coming in, I was tempted to hold onto it. Suddenly, you can feel like you have to save—every dime—when you should believe God like you did before.

God is saying, "Get your hands out of your pockets; I need some of those resources for My kingdom." But we say, "I would give, Lord, but I want to make sure it's You." That's selfish, not spiritual. When you were broke, you probably gave money to every homeless person on the street. Then when you have money you're tempted to say, "Well, I have to know that it's God before I give. I just have to make sure...he might use the money to buy drugs..."

What are you going to do, stand in front of that person until God answers you? Are you going to go home and come back the next day? If God is moving, *give*. Reach out. This is how to keep your harvest!

Say this out loud, "God wants me to be blessed."

Say it like you mean it—because He really does! It's His good pleasure to give you the kingdom...He loves to see you prosper. Remember Deuteronomy 8:18, "But thou shalt remember the LORD thy God: for ***it is* he** that giveth thee power to get wealth, that he may establish his covenant which he sware unto thy fathers..." (emphasis added).

God wants all of His children to be blessed—including you. Yet, in order to keep the blessing, you have to keep reaching out. Share the "fat of the land" with others.

- 61 -

Let Your Roots Go Deep

I preach the gospel so that you will be able to find what I've found in Christ, and that you would be blessed just as God has blessed me. In order to do this, you must learn how to stay in the realm of blessing. God called me to preach many years ago; and at first, I ran from the call. I ran because I needed validation. I needed so badly for somebody to accept me and to say something nice about me that I resisted doing what God needed me to do for His kingdom.

Whenever I'd get up to preach a Word that God had placed in my heart, other preachers would come against me saying things like, "Oh, no, brother, that isn't the way. God put cancer on that woman because He was trying to teach her something." What surprised me was that many of these people called themselves faith preachers!

Harvest Time: What's That All About?

So I ran. I didn't preach because I didn't want to be rejected. The praise and acceptance of man meant more to me than being in right standing with God. *In doing so, I was jeopardizing my harvest.* My roots desperately needed to go deeper in God, because I was living on topsoil. I needed to acknowledge Jesus as the anchor of my soul (see Hebrews 6:11–20). Listen to me. If you desperately need friends and family to pat you on your back and say good things to you, then you're in a good place for the devil to mess you up. Remember what Paul said in 2 Timothy 2:9–10…"Wherein [in the gospel] I suffer trouble, as an evil doer, *even* unto bonds; but the word of God is not bound. Therefore I endure all things…" (emphasis added).

If the prospect of receiving either praise or insults governs your life, God can't use you like He desires. I had to learn this…I had to be faithful and stable, whether people were saying good things about me or not. I had to stand and serve Him, whether they accepted or rejected me. You can't live your life needing to be affirmed and exalted by others (whether it's your wife, husband, mother, sister…anybody) in order to feel secure about who you are in the Lord. That's between you and God *alone*. Nobody should be able to influence you on that level except God. Nobody.

Gangs are growing today because people have no roots. This is how it happens. A gang member will approach an obviously insecure person (that needs praise from others) and say, "You're our family, you're our brother; we've got your back. Wear our colors as a sign of acceptance." Kids flock to it. Why do these same kids feel that they can't come into the body of Christ and receive that same acceptance and praise?

One thing I love about our church is that we're not critical. If I see this happening, I step on it fast. I don't care if we have 1,500 or 15,000 members—I won't stand by and let a slandering, backbiting spirit rise up among the people. It can start with something simple like, "Do you know what she did today?" The Bible says that if we don't have an edifying word, we shouldn't say anything. If you don't have something good to say, then don't say anything…*keep your mouth shut.* Trust in God—let your roots go deep.

As a people of God, our motivation to receive whatever blessing we're believing for should be "for the sake of the elect." Our harvest should feed, bless, and edify the entire body of Christ.

My wife can testify that when we were homeless and I was on my face crying out to God, He said to me, "I told you to go preach this

Harvest Principle IX: Sustain Your Land

word." I pleaded, "Give me a little more time. Nobody will listen to me..." God knew that I was seeking human validation. He said, "Go preach it anyway." Then He added, "I'm going to move on your behalf and bless you. I'm going to prosper you." Shortly afterwards, about seven or eight prophets from Africa (and other places around the world) started calling me and confirming that word.

One night, I got on my face before the Lord and said, "God, don't prosper me, just hear my prayer." Now, I knew this wasn't coming from my self-interest; something rose up within me while I was spending time with God. Then I heard more words coming out of my mouth that weren't at all like my personality, "God, don't prosper me and don't bless me unless You give me the ability to teach somebody else how to do the same thing; give me the anointing to communicate it in a way that other people can receive it. I don't want to prosper all by myself and see the rest of my brothers and sisters in poverty and hunger, not being able to get their needs met. I don't want anybody to look at me and say, 'God, why are You blessing him and You're not blessing me?' "

Know this: When God blesses one person and not another, it's not because He likes one better than the other. It happened because one person believed God and the other person didn't. One person let his or her roots go deep and the other stayed on the surface. It's that simple. When I let my roots go deeper in God and learned to obey His direction, it didn't matter what people said...and I've been reaping ever since.

- 62 -

Fight the "Good Fight"

Stop thinking that the harvest only comes for certain, "privileged" people...like pastors or other church leaders. God doesn't bless certain people more because they may have been saved longer than you have. The fact is, He'll step over a hundred million people who attend church regularly for one person who will simply believe. That's what Jesus did. In John 5:1–9, He walked by the Pool of Bethsaida, stepped over all of the people who were weak, blind, crippled, and withered, and went over to one man. After Jesus told that man to get up, He stepped right back out. Jesus didn't heal everybody at the pool. He went straight to one person and asked, "Will you be made whole?"

Harvest Time: What's That All About?

What about you? Are you ready to reap your harvest? First Timothy 6:12 says, "Fight the good fight of faith, lay hold on eternal life, whereunto thou art also called, and hast professed a good profession before many witnesses." This is why you don't have to struggle with the devil. The fight in which we're supposed to be engaged as children of God is the fight *of faith*, not a fight against the enemy. Jesus already defeated him over two thousand years ago—so we don't have to fight him today. According to James 4:7, we simply need to submit to God and resist the devil—then he must flee. When Jesus said, "It is finished," that's what He meant (see John 19:28–30).

We are fighting a *good fight* toward that which is good—not trying to get out of that which is evil. We fight to maintain what God has already obtained for us: first in our hearts, and then in our lives. Let's say you're in a house that belongs to you and somebody tries to come and take it. You know that you're within your rights to stay there. *That's the good fight.*

I've known people who were wimps; but even though they were weak and cowardly (avoiding all forms of confrontation), when they were attacked in the wrong area…and they knew they were right…fire came up from within them. "I'll kill you…you're trying to take what's mine!" That's how believers need to perceive the devil's position. In other words, we need to see our battle from the winning side (not from the perspective of trying to obtain). We need to *maintain* what we've already obtained that the devil is trying to steal.

Ephesians 6:10–13 says, "In conclusion, be strong in the Lord [be empowered through your union with Him]; draw your strength from Him [that strength which His boundless might provides]. Put on God's whole armor [the armor of a heavy-armed soldier which God supplies], that you may be able successfully to stand up against [all] the strategies *and* the deceits of the devil. For we are not wrestling with flesh and blood [contending only with physical opponents], but against the despotisms, against the powers, against [the master spirits who are] the world rulers of this present darkness, against the spirit forces of wickedness in the heavenly (supernatural) sphere. Therefore put on God's complete armor, that you may be able to resist *and* stand your ground on the evil day [of danger], and, having done all [the crisis demands], to stand [firmly in your place]" (Ampl.).

Picture it this way. Jesus is on the throne in heaven, the enemy is in the second heaven—and you're seated in "heavenly places" in Christ Jesus (Ephesians 2:6). This means you're way above the enemy's tactics. So he starts hurling accusations at you because he's trying to unseat you from your rightful place. However, you don't even

Harvest Principle IX: Sustain Your Land

have to look his way...because your armor *is, was,* and *always will be* complete in Christ. All you have to do is stand (in your place)...submit (by fighting the good fight of faith)...and resist. Do you see what I mean?

Say out loud, right now—"From now on, I'm going to fight the *good fight* of faith."

Now, let's go back to 1 Timothy 6:12..."Fight the good fight of faith, lay hold on eternal life, whereunto thou art also called, and hast professed a good profession before many witnesses." I want you to focus on two words, *lay hold.* This is the divine process. This is how you'll make it through every principle to receive your harvest from God. You must possess it. You must *lay hold* to eternal life every day remembering that it was given to you the moment you accepted Jesus Christ as Lord. You don't have to die to obtain eternal life; you already have it. When you *lay hold,* it's yours *now.* Jesus already purchased it for you—so fight the good fight...don't give up something that's rightfully yours!

This is why 2 Corinthians 5:8 says, "...To be absent from the body is to be present with the Lord." When the natural body dies, the process is immediate, because eternal life is already ours. This is the first part of our inheritance in Christ.

The Bible clearly says that God provides seed for the sower, bread for the eater, and a mighty harvest for anyone who is ready to reap it. We don't have to wrestle something out of God's hand that He doesn't want us to have. He has already provided what we need and more...it's up to us to go and get it. Imagine that God checked your coat and then left the ticket out somewhere for you to redeem it. You simply need to go and claim what's already there. Can you see the harvest? *It's white.* It's ready for the taking.

Don't make concessions with the devil. You know what he is like...if you give him an inch, he'll take a yard, a foot, a mile—he'll take everything that you surrender to him. The decision is yours. *Fight the good fight of faith and lay hold on eternal life...*Stand your ground, no matter what the devil is trying to steal from you. Let me say it again from James 4:7, "So be subject to God. Resist the devil [stand firm against him], and he will flee from you" (Ampl.).

The enemy can't steal your harvest if you've built on a strong foundation. Be a wise son or daughter of the kingdom. *Fight the good fight.* Plow your ground. Set the right atmosphere. Sow your seeds. Reap the harvest that God has already prepared for you from before the foundation of the world. Move forward on the word of the Lord, and you'll not only reap your harvest...you'll keep it.

Harvest Time: What's That All About?

Pray and Declare Your Harvest!

Bow your head with me in prayer. "Lord, I know that You have chosen us and are fully willing and able to keep us. Teach us to be strong in the revelation that will bring us total freedom. Your Word is truth. There is no darkness in You at all. We receive the light of the glorious truth, which has and will continue to make us free. Not one seed of Your Word will fall to the ground, failing to produce a harvest; instead, each seed will return to You having richly prospered in Your purpose. Thank You for giving us the opportunity to share in Your harvest field and to experience the power of Your faithfulness.

"In Jesus' name. Amen."

So be it.

So it must be.

HARVEST PRINCIPLE IX
EIGHT WAYS TO SUSTAIN YOUR LAND

Stand on the Word of God...Keep Your Ground
2 Tim. 2:8–10, Isa. 55:10–11, Eph. 6:13–18

Rest in the Lord...Let the Soil Rest
2 Tim. 2:10, Jn. 19:30

Remember the Lord during Times of Plenty...Lift Up Your Eyes
Deut. 8:12–14, Ps. 103:1–5

Remain Humble...Keep Your Head Covered
Deut. 8:13–18

Remain Instant...in Every Season
2 Tim. 4:2, Lk. 12:29 and 31, 2 Tim. 2:10

Reach Out to Others in Need
Prov. 11:25, Lk. 6:30–38, Deut. 8:18

Endure All Things...Let Your Roots Go Deep
2 Tim. 2:9–10, Heb. 6:11–20

Fight the "Good Fight" of Faith
1 Tim. 6:12, Eph. 6:10–13, Jms. 4:7

Recommended Resources

"The Laws of Prosperity"
Kenneth Copeland
Kenneth Copeland Ministries
www.kcm.org

"Rules of Reaping"
Keith Moore
Moore Life Ministries
www.moorelife.org

"Honor from God"
Kenneth Copeland
Kenneth Copeland Ministries
www.kcm.org

To purchase additional ministry products
by Pastor Wm. Di'Mon Brown
visit the Joshua and Caleb Ministries online store

HTTP://JCMINC.ORG

To invite Pastor Brown to minister at your church,
conference, or event, please contact:

Joshua and Caleb Ministries, Inc.
83 Winona Lakes
East Stroudsburg, PA 18301
(570) 588–7889

or send an email request to:

REQUESTS@JCMINC.ORG